Cognizers

The Wiley Science Editions

Cognizers

Neural Networks

and

Machines That Think

R. Colin Johnson
Chappell Brown

Illustrated by
Lisa Metzger

WILEY

Wiley Science Editions
John Wiley & Sons, Inc.
New York • Chichester • Brisbane • Toronto • Singapore

Publisher: Stephen Kippur
Editor: David Sobel
Managing Editors: Andrew Hoffer and Corinne McCormick
Editing, Design, & Production: Publications Development Co., Crockett, Texas

Library of Congress Cataloging-in-Publication Data

Johnson, R. Colin.
    Cognizers : neural networks and machines that think / R. Colin Johnson, Chappell Brown.
        p.   cm. — (Wiley science editions)
    Bibliography: p. 249
    ISBN 0-471-61161-1
    1. Neural computers. 2. Artificial intelligence.   I. Brown, Chappell. II. Title. III. Series.
QA76.5.J585   1988
006.3—dc19   88-17387
                                                     CIP

Printed in the United States of America

88 89 10 9 8 7 6 5 4 3 2

When I conceived of **Cognizers**,
I was an executive editor at
Electronic Engineering Times.
I had a hard time getting reporters interested
in the "wet-ware" of the brain.
Luckily, I was able to capture
the imagination of Chappell Brown.

But more than anyone else,
this book would not have been
possible without Lisa Metzger.

Lisa not only provided the
illustrations for **Cognizers**, but also
kept me going through the endless revisions
that were necessary to make sure
this book accurately represents
the state-of-the-art
in such a quickly changing field.

Thank you, Lisa.

cognizer \ käg- ˈnīz-ər\ n.

synonym for synthetic neural network
< *the cognizer solved the problem without computing* >
(back formation from cognizance)

cognizance \ˈkäg-ne -zən(t)s\, n.
from cognition: the process of knowing,
including both awareness and judgment

cognize \käg-ˈniz\ vt. -nized; -nizing:
to perceive something for the first time
< *to cognize the new concept took some time* >

recognize \ˈrek-ig-nīz\ vt. -nized; -nizing:
to perceive something previously known
< *to recognize it again was quite easy* >

Preface

It was one of the larger lecture halls to accommodate all the people. Five minutes to go and the place was anything but reverently silent. The air was alive with anticipation. "There he is," someone said and applause spontaneously broke out from previous attendees of professor Frank Rosenblatt's lectures at Cornell University.

The subject of his lectures was "perceptrons"—machines that could perceive and learn from their environment. "At first we did not believe him, but when you found out how he was doing it, you knew he had discovered a general purpose recognition technology," recalls David Ripps, then a chemical engineering undergraduate at Cornell.

A machine that could recognize anything, from handwriting to faces, seemed a long way off for the budding computer community in 1958. That drove people to pack his lectures and wildly speculate about his discovery. In those days computers were sometimes called "electronic brains," but Rosenblatt's perceptron seemed even more akin to the neural networks of the brain than a computer.

Rosenblatt looked almost embarrassed at being so well received as he waved them to silence so that he could begin. "He was much more conservative than those who were in the audience," Ripps revealed. "He was not making great claims for the perceptron, but rather that he was investigating it in an orderly way."

Nevertheless the mimeographed copy of his manuscript "Principles of Neurodynamics: Perceptrons and the Theory of Brain Mechanisms," always seemed to be in use in Cornell's

Library. They did not allow it to circulate until it was published in 1961.

Like many of his colleagues of the era, Ripps subsequently turned to computer engineering rather than neural networks. Ripps is now vice president of Industrial Programming Inc., Jericho, New York. He never worked in the field of neural networks, "but I have never forgotten those lectures and have often wondered what became of Rosenblatt's research," Ripps mused.

Today that research is alive and well and experiencing a resurgence. Once again the spirit of discovery is packing lecture halls and overflowing impromptu meetings and conferences. Five years ago there were no major conferences devoted to the subject. In 1986 the National Science Foundation sponsored the first open conference devoted to neural networks. The one room affair was packed to standing room only, because no one expected such a large turnout. In 1987 the Institute of Electrical and Electronic Engineers sponsored the first well publicized conference. They expected less than 500 attendees, but over 1600 showed up. In 1988 more than one conference per month was scheduled including the debut meeting of the freshly formed International Neural Network Society.

But just what are these "neural networks" that are generating such widespread interest? This book traces the history of neural networks as an alternative to traditional computing devices. In particular, it concentrates on the variety of neural networks that do not merely simulate the brain with software on conventional computers, but which truly model the brain in a synthetic medium—cognizers.

R. COLIN JOHNSON
SEPT. 13, 1988

Contents

Introduction

The computer revolution is running up against the fundamental limits of the principles upon which it is based. The serial one-step-at-a-time pace of "computation" has produced some remarkable computers, but nothing that can compare to the human brain.

■■■ This book is about machines that are modeled on the brain: *cognizers*. Unlike the brain, computers separate memory functions from computation and use software to glue the two back together, albeit, one datum at a time. The bottleneck caused by one processor using data items only one at a time is choking traditional computation. The brain, on the other hand, processes many continuous streams of information coming in from the senses, by uniting memory and information processing.

Computers generally depend upon a single central processing unit (CPU) to perform each processing task, one step at a time. "Parallel" processors (also called concurrent processors), harness the power of many central processing units simultaneously to relieve this bottleneck. However, parallel processing has become bogged down with the problem of communications among these units. The machines work masterfully on problems that utilize each processor for a different task, in addition, techniques for partitioning some scientific problems have been found. But there are no established principles revealing how to automate the arduous manual task of partitioning any real-world problem so that it can be parcelled out to many processors simultaneously.

Attempts to simulate brainlike functions on conventional computers—artificial intelligence (AI)—have proven successful in noncritical settings. *Expert systems*, for example, are computer programs that encapsulate a relatively small specialized domain of knowledge and provide a programmable "inference engine" for using it. Unfortunately, expert systems require knowledge engineers who are smart enough to specify a response to every possible circumstance with which the AI system might be faced. In a closed environment where there are well-defined answers for every question, that is possible. In the real world, however, it would take an omniscient programmer to anticipate every possible combination of circumstances with which an expert system might have to deal.

When an expert system is taken outside the narrow, well-defined domain for which it was designed, it invariably fails. Some researchers propose that increasingly larger amounts of computing power are all that are needed to widen the scope of AI systems. However, expert systems already evaluate thousands or even millions of high-level psychological constructs in order to mimic a single human conclusion. It is my contention that this approach is ultimately bankrupt.

Together computer science and AI have reached the limits of the principles upon which they are based. If computers are to transcend the bottleneck that is limiting their growth, engineers must employ new principles that can synchronize many different operations simultaneously. Similarly, if AI is to be successful in unrestricted domains—such as autonomous vehicles—new principles must be found for simultaneously juggling thousands of opposing alternatives. Finally, if parallel processing is to become possible on a scale large enough to allow it to deal with real-life problems, a way must be found to connect the processors simply and efficiently. The answers to these problems are not likely to come from computer scientists or AI researchers. Rather, neuroscientists may hold the key.

The Brain Does Many Things at Once

The brain distributes its processing tasks among billions of relatively unintelligent nerve cells called *neurons*. It routinely handles communications among these billions of neurons, each one of which is sending and receiving information constantly. In the 1950s, a few visionaries believed that studying the brain might unearth principles needed to transcend the bottleneck presented by a central processing unit. After 25 years, that dream is coming to pass.

A number of brain mechanisms have been unraveled, each one of which solves certain problems of simultaneous processing. These mechanisms include association, generalization, and self-organization. Each of these principles can direct the simultaneous action of many separate neural processors towards a common goal. Unfortunately, these principles have been found to be irreducible to the lock-step serial processing characteristic of computers. Millions of microcomputers could be connected in the pattern of neural networks in the brain, but the tasks that real neurons perform cannot be duplicated. The neuron's multifunctional abilities are just too different from the computational capabilities of digital computers to make this solution effective.

Neural networks in the brain process information according to noncomputational principles. Neurons perform continuous operations, as opposed to the discrete operations of digital computers. One aspect of neurons—their continuous nature—can be simulated with computer software, as is done in neurocomputers, but within the next 10 years, truer models of brain mechanisms will emerge using especially designed neural-like microchips.

The Brain Is Not a Computer

Though digital computers are being used to simulate the information processing of the brain, machines that truly model the brain, rather than merely simulate it, substitute noncomputational physical mechanisms for the logic and mathematics of computation.

Some scientists maintain that the neural networks of the brain and of the machines modeled on the brain are really just analog, as opposed to digital, computers. Before digital-computers dominated automation, they competed against analog computers that did not use the discrete values of digital logic. But other than using continuous numerical values, these analog computers bore little similarity to the brain. Based on the same one-step-at-a-time constraints that have shackled digital computation, they did not attempt to model any of the the global evaluation capabilities of the brain. They were forced to follow a program just like their digital counterparts.

Computers, no matter what the technology in which they are cast, are based on the same reductionist approach to problem solving. It is precisely that approach that must be discarded in order to build the synthetic neural networks of the future. Thus, because they employ principles that are antithetical to the reductionism on which all computation is based, I have chosen to call these new machines *cognizers*.*

Roots of Reductionism

Reductionism, as I define it, has been gathering strength ever since it first appeared in Euclid's *Elements* around 300 B.C. Euclid's axiomatic geometry demonstrated to the world that truth could be codified with the deductive power of logic. In such systems, a set of objects are operated upon by common notions—well-known formulae called axioms—to yield truths about the world. For instance, geometric objects like lines and angles are coupled with axioms like "the sum of a triangle's angles is 180°" to yield truths such as "if two of the angles of this triangle sum to 120°, then the third must be 60°."

In Euclid's day, geometry was thought to encompass all such formal systems about truths in the world. A non-Euclidean geometry would have been a contradiction in terms. Over the ages, reductionists have followed Euclid's lead and slowly replaced the various causal connections in the world with the deductive power of axiomatic formalisms. Ordinary causality, as learned by experiencing the world, has lost its explanatory power in favor of implication within formal systems. However, since cognizers mark a return to dependence upon causality, causal connections are what they learn.

*I am indebted to professor Robert Rosen and his chapter in *Real Brains, Artificial Minds* (Elsevier, 1987) for helping to clarify these issues for me.

Formal systems begin with structureless elementary atoms as a basis from which to describe the various aspects of a given problem. Axioms are then suggested and conclusions drawn by implication. If the predictions are born out in the world, then the axioms are strengthened. If not, then the atoms or axioms are revised and new predictions made. Philosophers of science have endlessly debated the proper methodologies for verifying or falsifying such systems. But throughout, they accept the basic tenet that *formalisms model the world*. With a good set of axioms for a given problem, so the reductionist argues, the causal connections between objects in the world can be replaced by logical implication within a formal system.

But is any "truth" lost in formal systems? Can it really be that all the meaning (semantics) of learned descriptions of the world is preserved in the scant atoms and logic (syntax) of a formal system? Pure syntax—the postulated atoms, hypothesized axioms, and the deductive power of implication—is a long way from the sounds and sights, the pains and pleasures of living experience. The textured, semantic content in learned descriptions of causality in the world does not jibe well with the featureless expanse of purely syntactic descriptions. Geometry, for instance, pictures the world as points and lines and planes. But these are empty structures when compared to red balls, laser beams, and asphalt parking lots.

Nevertheless, reductionists hold that no truth is lost by replacing real-world causality with logical implication. Nearly 2000 years after Euclid, the seventeenth-century philosopher René Descartes argued that the only thing learned experience of the world could yield for sure was *Cogito Ergo Sum*—*I think, therefore I am*. This ultimate atom of truth reduced to chimera all mere causal connections experienced in the world. Luckily, there was no longer a need for causality, because implication in a formal system could replace it. The rest of reality could be deduced from the bare existence of the "I" in *Cogito Ergo Sum*. According to Descartes, pure syntax lost no meaning.

One immediate consequence of this reformulation of causality was the introduction of *fate*. If the past implies the future, then events must be determined in advance. All scientists needed to do was find the suitable formalism, and then by implication, the past could foretell the future. The formalist merely required that the world be encoded as syntactic objects (atoms) and that the proper axioms (natural laws) be encoded as propositions about those objects. Causality among the objects in the world could then be replaced with propositions about syntactic objects. The conclusions deduced by such implication could subsequently be decoded as truths about objects in the world. The search for natural law thus became an attempt to bring the causal relations in the external world into congruence with implication relations in a suitable formalism.

In the eighteenth century, reductionism was challenged by inquiries into the basis of mathematics and by the discovery of non-Euclidean geometries. Which of the many alternative geometries was the real one? How could truth in the world be deduced if incompatible formal systems could each describe learned experience? Was only one system really true? Were they all equally true? If truth was relative, then what did that imply about determinism? These questions injected an unexpected indeterminism into the budding reductionist community, prompting logicians to pursue questions about the consistency and completeness of formal systems in general.

The usual reductionist ploy—searching for smaller atoms—was vigorously pursued in order to sew back together the fragmented remnants of the many possible worlds. In the latter part of the nineteenth century, Georg Cantor created just such a common ground with his set theory, in which formal systems could each be represented. At first, mathematical deduction appeared to be forever secured by Cantor's all encompassing formalism—the pristine exemplar of reductionism.

However, critics later devised glaring paradoxes from self-referential propositions and other anomalies that tainted set theory's unifying power. These criticisms of set theory, however, were laid to rest by logicians like Gottlob Frege, Bertrand Russell, and, much later, Willard Van Orman Quine. These men eliminated paradoxes by blaming them on the remnants of semantics lurking within propositions. By purging all traces of semantics from formalisms, implication was reinstated as the true successor to learned experience of causality. Consider Quine's restatement of *Cogito Ergo Sum:* To be is to be the value of a variable in logic.

Computers Automated Formal Systems

Once a scientific theory was formalized within the correct system, the investigation of it was at first thought to be a mechanical process, something a machine could do. In 1936, Alan Turing presented just such a mechanical version of a syntactic engine—an ideal computing machine that could automatically deduce conclusions within a formalism. Humans no longer had to manipulate slavishly the meaningless symbols in formal systems—a Turing machine could do it. This ideal computer has become the main reductionist tool for scientific inquiry.

Turing modeled his machine's operations on simple arithmetic calculations called effective processes. An *algorithm* was the formal counterpart of an effective process and was defined as the rote process of applying to propositions the syntactic production rules of a formal theory. A computer *program* was subsequently defined as a sequence of algorithms. If the program ever stopped when supplied with certain input data, then the resulting conclusion was said to be true, that is, a *theorem* in the formal system.

Turing asked himself whether a general-purpose universal computer program could exist in which any formal theory could be encoded and all truths be automatically deduced. Such a machine would be the reductionist's fondest dream because it could automate the entire process of deducing truths from axioms. Alas, Turing's question was rhetorical since the logician Kurt Gödel had already shown in 1931 that logically such a formulation would forever be incomplete, even for the effective processes of basic arithmetic. Gödel had shown that no matter what set of axioms and postulates are chosen to formalize arithmetic, there will always be some theorems that are true but which cannot be derived purely syntactically. Turing applied this conclusion, showing that there was no way to program a computer so that it could tell, on purely syntactic grounds, whether a given proposition was a theorem or not. In essence, Turing's "undecidability" theorem is that no formal system can hold the whole truth. Different formal systems can harbor different gaps in coverage, but no one formal system can contain it all.

However, this residue of semantic content did not resist formalization for long. A contemporary of Turing, logician Alonzo Church, seemingly eliminated that residue for any particular application. It was true that a universal program could not be fashioned to deduce all the truths implicit in a formalism, but, most importantly, any *particular* effective process could be replaced by a program. Church's thesis was that an algorithm could always replace any effective process that worked in the world. Mathematically speaking, Church implied that any causal sequence could be represented by a corresponding recursive process—that is, a finite sequence of algorithms that refer to nothing outside themselves, or as *Webster's Ninth New Collegiate Dictionary* defines recursive, "a procedure that can repeat itself indefinitely or until a specified condition is met."

Church's thesis fueled anew the reductionists' furor. Newtonian mechanics was formalized into the states of particles and laws of dynamics. Particles were said to be structureless syntactic objects whose only attributes were the parameters of position and velocity; these objects inhabited a configuration space, just as the symbols submitted to a formal computer do. The forces that push these ultimate units around were the precise analogs of the algorithms in a formal computer. Even post-Newtonian physicists like Niels Bohr have argued that quantum theory is only a formal mathematical engine and that any attempt to imbue it with specific meaning (semantic content) is an inherently self-contradictory endeavor.

Modeling versus Simulating

By coupling George Boole's particular digital characterization of logic with Turing's seminal machine, John von Neumann implemented the modern computer. Thus the computer, be it digital or analog, was expressly designed to automate the reductionist method of replacing causality among objects in the world with implications among propositions about syntactic objects. A computer program encodes the problem to be solved as syntactic objects and axiomatic propositions about the application. The program is then run and, when it halts, its results are decoded as truths about the world. As such, the computer's most basic utility lies in its capacity to simulate formal systems.

It is precisely the reductionist aspect of computation that makes it unsuitable for synthetic neural networks, or what I call *cognizers*. Though the computer's capacity to simulate is of great practical utility, it can not model the world as cognizers do because it is constrained to follow the formal dictates of its programming. In common usage, the terms *model* and *simulate* are often used interchangeably. But it is precisely this distinction between modeling and simulating which makes it difficult to call synthetic neural networks any kind of computer.

Although computer simulations can produce artificial neural networks with artificial intelligence, they will never produce genuine synthetic intelligence. Like a steak made of wax in a restaurant's display window, neural-network simulations are not genuine. But a synthetic steak, perhaps made from soy beans, is just as edible as a real one and thus just as genuine as a synthetic neural network that truly models the brain.

I have already shown, in my description of the origins of computation, how a simulation of the world was formalized by substituting implication for causation. In contrast, a model makes no such substitution but instead mirrors in a *synthetic* system the causal features of the *natural* system. For instance, a *simulation* of a bridge collapsing will encode the stress (S) and the breaking point (BP) as syntactic variables in a computer program. Thus

S > BP→ print Bridge Collapsed means that if the stress exceeds the breaking point, then the bridge will collapse. In contrast to a simulation, a model of the bridge in miniature will use physical materials whose breaking point matches the scaled-weight applied to the full-sized bridge. The model uses actual rather than simulated stress.

Simulations merely attempt to encode the causal features of a natural system in a formal system and cancel out the causal features of the synthetic system itself—that is, the computer running the simulation. All relevant features of the material system are expressed as software in the computer. In contrast, the model's physical makeup, such as the "breaking point," is central to its ability to model. But the simulating computer's physical structure itself encodes nothing: it merely automates the effective processes that could have been carried out by hand, such as working out the implications of:

$$S = 10, \; BP = 9 \text{ and } If \; (S > BP) \rightarrow print \; Bridge \; Collapsed.$$

Neither simulating nor modeling can mimic every aspect of the system being modeled, but the modeling relation is generally transitive, whereas simulation is not. That is, if A is a model of B and B is a model of C, then A is also generally a model of C. For instance, say A is a miniature replica of a suspension bridge, B is the Golden Gate Bridge and C is the San Francisco skyline. Transitivity means that because the replica is a model of the Golden Gate Bridge, and the Golden Gate Bridge is a model of the San Francisco skyline, then the replica of the bridge is also a model of the San Francisco skyline.

Simulations, in general, fail the transitivity test—that is, if A is a simulation of B and B is a simulation of C, then A is generally *not* an simulation of C but a simulation of a simulation. For example, say that C is the county race track, B is a simulated race track on a slot machine, and A is a simulation of the slot machine that tells you how to bet. The physical race track is not simulated by the bet-placing simulation, because it is simulating how a slot machine works (gears, cogs, and microchips) and not how the county race track works (horses, dirt, and money). It is a simulation of a simulation and nothing more.

Simulations must follow their predetermined programs or face being wrong. A computer that concludes something other than what the formal system would conclude is said to be in error and is modified until its results do match that of the formal system. But a miniature bridge collapsing before the full-scale bridge is expected to fall would not be said to be wrong because models have no predetermined program and often reveal new aspects of problems not even previously considered.

A model bridge can collapse early because of inadequate detail or inappropriate materials in the model as well as for unforeseen defaults in the full-sized bridge. Simulations can similarly have inadequate detail or inappropriate algorithms that foil their ability to predict accurately. However, only the model can reveal unforeseen defaults; it genuinely mimics physical processes for what they are by casting them into another medium.

By replacing causality with implication, formal computer models imbue reductionism with the fatalistic determinism that is its Achilles' heel. The closer reductionist physicists scrutinize matter, the more subatomic particles they require to explain what they perceive there. The closer reductionists looks at biology, the more cell theory is broken down into molecular units and programmable genetics. All these reductionist schemes to explain complex mechanisms as aggregates of simple mechanisms under axiomatic rule are doomed to fail, especially when applied to complex phenomena in biology. Rather, scientists are increasingly finding that complex problems involve nonlinear combinations of shifting causal connections that defy determinism.

For instance, no matter how big a computer simulation of the weather is run, it will never predict very far into the future.* The reductionist would say that a sufficiently detailed simulation could achieve predictions for any arbitrary number of days into

*See James Gleick's *Chaos—Making A New Science* (Viking, 1987).

the future merely by using increasingly larger computer simulations for more days. But the complex causal structure of the weather will never allow predictions very far into the future; causes come in too many different varieties and interact in too nonlinear a manner to make accurate predictions possible. Scientists call this phenomenon *chaos*.

Complex causal interactions yield an objective explanation for every event at the time it occurs. But this explanation does not imply the fatalistic conclusion that everything in the future is determined by the past. Chaos theory teaches that causality cannot be used to predict events very far into the future because nonlinear interactions shift the causal structure as it develops. Each event has an objective cause, but the further one extrapolates from the present situation into the future, the less reliable are the predictions.

Entrée Biology

It is the complex causal interactions within cognizers that distinguish them from computer simulations. Cognizers are true models of living nervous systems, cast in the electronics medium. A simulation is constrained to move from state to state according to the deterministic dictates of its programming, but a cognizer does not have a set of states. It transcends determinism by using the same causal connections that brains do. Accordingly, cognizers promise to exhibit genuinely intelligent behavior, albeit in a synthetic organism.

The study of neural networks began with reductionist simulations such as those of Warren McCulloch and Walter Pitts, who in 1943 proposed networks of formal neurons that exhibited the brainlike behaviors of learning, categorizing, and remembering (see Chapter 2). McCulloch and Pitts showed that formal components, basically digital switches with thresholds, could replace a Turing machine. Since the Turing machine is the foundation on which digital computers are based, McCulloch and Pitts in effect showed that a formal neural network could simulate brain activity on a digital computer by using an appropriate program. Artificial intelligence is similarly founded.

But cognizers are not constrained to adhere to a formal system. Rather they act in accordance with causal relations among their constituent physical systems and thus can truly model real neural networks. Cognizers perceive semantic content in precisely the same manner that humans do—that is, by learning from experience. What they learn about are the causal connections among objects so that they can generalize in the future with intelligence wrought from the past (see Chapter 4).

The thoughts of humans signify their proper objects because they are derived from experiences of those objects. Cognizers also derive the meaning of objects from their perceptions of them. Their subsequent memories of those objects thus possess an intentionality that defines the semantic content of their internal states in a manner that no computer can ever simulate. Church's thesis rightly claims that computer programs constitute a class of universal *simulators* for material processes, even biological processes. But Church's thesis does not apply to complex systems like cognizers which express both syntactic and semantic content in precisely the same manner as humans. Their syntax is causation and their semantics comes from learning (see Chapter 5).

Computation Redefined

Reductionist scientists have attempted to compare computers to electronic circuitry modeled on the brain, pointing out that the electronic technologies used to build them are similar: after all, each uses transistor-based microchips. However someone using this style of argument could prove that anything composed of transistors, such as an AM radio, is really a computer (see Chapter 6).

By redefining the term computation, other reductionist scientists have argued that the brain and synthetic neural networks built to emulate it are really computers. If one defines computation to encompass what brains do, then brains are computers by definition. These scientists use terms such as computational neuroscience for what I would call the study of neural simulations. They maintain that computers start with initial conditions, move through a series of states and come to rest in a final condition called the answer. Likewise, these scientists argue, the neural networks of the brain start with initial conditions, move through a series of states and come to rest in a final condition called the answer. Consequently this argument merely broadens the definition of computer so as to dilute its meaning beyond recognition. Under this analysis, flipping a coin to decide between two choices becomes a computation and the coin is a computer. Similarly, spinning a bottle to see who goes next in a game becomes a computation while the bottle is a computer.

Intuitively, these redefinitions make some small sense, but careful consideration reveals that this small sense is not worth the grave consequences it entails. Defining what the brain does as collective computation ignores the fact that brains solve problems in a manner *different* from computers, a fact which explains why technologists began studying the brain as a model for thinking machines in the first place.

Neural networks in the brain use principles like association, generalization and self-organization to evaluate simultaneously the many aspects of a problem. These networks enable the brain to solve problems that, for computers, are intractable—that is, would take an incredible amount of computer time to solve. Clearly, some of the problems that the brain solves routinely will *never* be simulated on a computer. Somehow, the brain is harnessing chaos to solve problems, whereas computers are limited by determinism.

But What Do We Call Them?

So far, this introduction has been a rather long description of how I came to call this book *Cognizers*. To call synthetic neural networks any kind of computer, such as biocomputers, implied that the brain was also some sort of a computer. Representing cognition, be it natural or synthetic, as computation was so repugnant and so dehumanizing to me that I had to find a viable alternative. After delving into the issues, I became convinced that it also made good scientific sense to find a more accurate alternative.

But to refer to these new machines with the cumbersome phrase *synthetic neural networks* posed equally difficult literary problems. The main problem is that the noun phrase *synthetic neural network* has no verb form whereas *computer* is a noun, *compute* is a verb, and variations like *computing* express the action of *computation*. Thus the word computer is not only descriptive, but also flexible. *Synthetic neural network*, on the other hand, describes the structure of machines modeled after the brain, but not the actions that they perform.

What word, then, could be both descriptive and flexible enough to express action as well? As a starting point, I took it as given that synthetic neural networks are built to model human cognition. After consulting *Webster's Ninth New Collegiate Dictionary* for derivatives of *cognition*, I arrived upon the word *cognizer.* * It is both a noun denoting that which exhibits cognition and a verb. Just as *computer* has *compute* and *computation* as derivatives, *cognizer* is related to *cognize* and *cognition*.

Cognizer is derived from the root cognizance. It first appeared in general usage around 1836, according to *Webster's Ninth New Collegiate Dictionary*, though *Random House's Second Unabridged Dictionary of the English Language* claims to have found usages as early as 1640. As a noun, cognizer can be applied to anything that exhibits the elements of cognition. Any human that is cognizant is a cognizer, just as computer was once a title for anyone who performed manual calculations. A machine is a cognizer to the extent that it performs the same sort of cognitive functions as a human.

Cognizer also has the convenient relative *recognize*. To recognize, according to *Webster's Ninth New Collegiate Dictionary*, is to perceive something that was previously known. Thus to cognize

---

Webster's Ninth New Collegiate Dictionary, p. 257.

is to perceive something for the first time. Though this meaning was not apparent to me when I chose cognizer, as this book has unfolded, it has worked out very conveniently.

One of the basic mechanisms in all cognizers is the act of cognizing itself. That act is performed each time a cognizer's awareness is turned toward a new object. At that time raw sensation is associated with memories of the past. If a match is found, that is called recognizing; if no match is found, a novel perception can be formed. This act of cognizing is precisely that which AI systems lack. Cognizers, whether fleshy or metallic, have an ability to organize their own internal representations of the world around them. They take in new experiences and store them away in their own internal memories. That is cognizing. But they can similarly bring stored memories once again into consciousness by association. That is recognizing.

I use the word cognizer because I need a word that denotes machines modeled on human cognition. Cognizer is not a coined word, like biocomputer, and it doesn't degrade the brain by suggesting that it is really a computer. Best of all, it has a rich variety of forms perfect for expressive writing.

1

Edge of the Frontier

Computer Science Needs a Unifying Theory

The computer revolution is running up against fundamental physical limits. Without new strategies, conventional architectures simply can not cope with the increasing complexity of systems. Mankind faces the edge of a frontier that it is ill-equipped to cross.

However, all is not lost. Several promising lines of research are converging on an alternative to computing that thrives on complexity rather than chokes on it.

Machines modeled on the structure of living nerve networks can augment digital circuitry to increase incrementally its power. It is hoped that such cognizers will vastly outperform computers, especially in matters of understanding and judgment.

Though they have reshaped society, digital computers are, in fact, based on age-old innovations. Although computers grew out of the need to calculate more accurately and quickly, society, particularly the merchant segment, found other uses for computers such as information processing and data transmission. These newer uses enhance other aspects of the computer that were implicit in its design, aspects like the use of a small alphabet to represent a large realm of ideas and instant access to on-line information.

The language of the computer is derived from George Boole's book, *An Investigation of the Laws of Thought*, written in 1854. Boole rocked nineteenth-century mathematics by proposing that logical expressions were computable. Though Boole had no college degree, he nevertheless demonstrated that algebraic methods could be applied to logic.

By integrating mathematical methods with logic, Boole demonstrated that ordinary problems in everyday life could be posed and solved by automata. Boole himself believed that he had found a connection between ordinary algebra and language that was attributable to a higher logic, which Boole called the laws of thought. Boolean logic is now universally used in digital computers.

Boole did not formulate his laws from any practical motivation; he simply felt that his work was uncovering the mysteries of the mind. His simplified calculus seemed useless in the context of nineteenth-century England, where the industrial revolution was charging ahead at full throttle. The machinery of the age used new metal refining techniques that allowed a strength and precision never achieved by craftsman of earlier ages while a universal power source—steam—made the wheels and gears turn at unprecedented speeds. Although Boole and his fellow logicians may have tapped into the fundamental laws of thought, they could not cast these ephemeral thoughts into steel.

Another innovator, looking for direct means to automate computation, took his cue from the machinery of the times. Charles Babbage had the vision to see that the methods by which looms were programmed to produce an endless variety of colorful patterns could be adapted to generate solutions to an endless list of problems. Babbage made a heroic attempt to build steam-driven machinery that could be supplied with a description of mathematical problems and then weave the answer.

Babbage was on the right track, as far as building a workable computational device, but his colorful and irascible personality doomed the project. He could not accept the limitations of contemporary technology and continually argued with his foreman, nor could he fathom the intricacies of the government bureaucracies that were funding the project. The analytical engine that he had imagined and designed in great detail would have worked, but at the end of his life, it stood unfinished.

Babbage's partial success showed that computation could be automated. Business machine companies began to offer information-processing products of more modest design. These new machines relied on punched cards, pegs, and gears to record and process information. The United States census began to rely on these methods, and by the 1920s the growth of the population and the variety of information collected on each citizen made these methods essential to the census process.

In the 1930s, the mechanical approach to computation reached its peak with a project at the Massachusetts Institute of Technology to build what were called differential analyzers. These analyzers relied on gear ratios to represent numerical operations and were set up specifically to integrate mathematical functions. They were also enormous machines weighing hundreds of tons, and very few were built. At the beginning of World War II, they became the sole computing resource of the War Department.

However, a more subtle approach to computation kept percolating in the minds of inventors. At the turn of the century, Nikola Tesla, a brilliant electromagnetic theorist and unconventional thinker, designed and patented an electronic logic gate that could be used to represent Boole's logical system. This gate, however, was only one of many of Tesla's ideas, and he never pursued applications of it.

Seminal Turing Machines

Though Boole and Tesla set the stage for computing machinery based on electronic logic, it took Alan Turing's mathematical definition of computation to bring them into being. Turing was attempting a model for computation that would be both precise and as general as possible. That meant that his definition would have to include all known forms of computation and anticipate any new approaches that might be devised in the future.

His definition has proven to be durable indeed. All of the

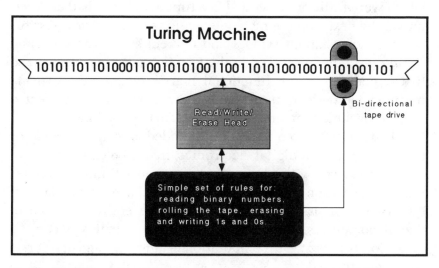

Turing Machine. Alan Turing's simplified machine proved to the world that a finite alphabet (say, 1s and 0s) and a simple set of rules could be used to solve any conceivable mathematical problem by merely reading, erasing, and writing symbols on an infinitely long tape.

machines that have come out of the computer revolution have been special cases of the abstract machine Turing conceived in 1936. Even the most experimental, parallel processors which harness multitudes of separate microprocessors simultaneously, are still based on Turing's model.

Turing's basic approach is simple, if somewhat abstract. He reasoned that any computation would have to consist of a sequence of clearly defined effective processes—automated versions of pencil-and-paper operations. The problem itself would be encoded in some alphabet of symbols, although the specific type of symbols was not important. He postulated a machine that could identify symbols in such an alphabet and manipulate them according to a few simple rules. The machine could read from and write to an external tape; it also could advance the tape forward or backward. A special symbol told the machine when to end a computation, and the internal workings of the machine itself were also encoded as a set of laws that described its operation—its axioms.

Any specific Turing machine had only one set of axioms, which were finite and encoded in a functional matrix that determined the next step the machine would take under any possible combination of input symbol and current state. The universal Turing machine, discussed in the *Introduction*, was designed so that it could read the functional matrix of any other Turing machine and perform those same operations. It was, in effect, a Turing machine that simulated other Turing machines.

This definition of computation provided an essential idea for the development of digital electronics: that problems can be encoded and solved with a limited set of symbols. Digital computer builders seized on this idea in its simplest form: an alphabet of only two symbols—1 and 0—provides the entire language of digital computers. George Boole's logical calculus became a guide for organizing a computational language and its corresponding circuits.

By easing the task of building actual devices to imitate Turing's abstraction, that drastic simplification helped the fledgling technology grow and develop. Digital devices need only to distinguish between two signal levels. Manufacturers compensate for this simplification by stamping out large numbers of devices cheaply so that incredibly complex configurations can be encoded by designers. This capability has continually enlarged the size and range of problems that can be effectively described and solved on computers.

Von Neumann Architecture

Still, it took a visionary leader who was mystified by how the mind reasons to see how Turing's principles could be taken as a blueprint for an electronic computer.

Though credited as being the father of digital computing, von Neumann was in fact convinced that he was modeling the brain. He considered building machines that accurately modeled the nerve impulse, but concluded that they would be too cumbersome to manufacture. The most radical of his proposed designs was based on a principle called pulse density in which numbers

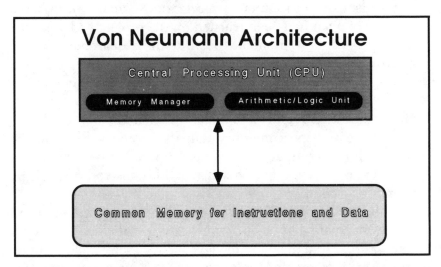

Von Neumann's Architecture. Father of the digital computer, John von Neumann showed how Turing's machine could be made practical by using a central-processing unit as the tape reader/writer and a common memory to store both instructions and data.

are represented by the frequency of pulses. A number was determined by counting pulses over time, and elaborate hardware was needed to perform even simply arithmetic operations.

The rise of the electronic age during war time swept von Neumann into the vortex of modern technology. He had already established a brilliant reputation in mathematics and its applications when a fateful encounter on a train platform changed the direction of his career.

An administrator of the top-secret Eniac project at the University of Pennsylvania's Moore School of Electrical Engineering recognized von Neumann and struck up a conversation with him. He boasted that engineers at the school had built an electronic device that could perform 300 arithmetic operations in one second. He was surprised when von Neumann became very animated, firing a barrage of technical questions about the machine. Since von Neumann already had security clearance, he was invited to visit the engineers on the project. After that encounter, the idea of electronic computation increasingly preoccupied his thoughts.

After his visit to the Eniac project, von Neumann prepared a summary of what had been learned on the project and what the next appropriate step should be. But the researchers on the Eniac project did not feel that they needed von Neumann's help because they had already formed a design for a new computer, which they were calling the Edvac. They had perceived the essential innovation required to make their first model more flexible, the creation of a memory unit that could store both the numbers for a computation along with its instructions. The Eniac did not have memory for instructions; instead it had to be rewired for each different kind of calculation.

A common memory for instructions (programs) and numbers is the essence of what has become known as the von Neumann architecture. From the point of view of a von Neumann machine, information is all treated the same, as binary strings of 1s and 0s. To produce desired results, only the human programmer need know the different instructions and data. Like Turing's machine, the operation of von Neumann's computer could be represented in the same Boolean alphabet as the numbers being operated on.

But von Neumann's suggestions for the next project went far beyond just adding a memory for instructions, called programs. The paper was widely distributed and had a profound effect on computer builders in the United States and Britain, including Alan Turing himself. Turing immediately saw how the basic design could be redesigned for higher speeds and talked the British government into funding a project. A working prototype was built, and for a short while it was the fastest computer in the world.

Since the Eniac project had been kept a secret, von Neumann's paper was viewed as the original blueprint for electronic computer design. Every computer up to the present has followed these basic design principles, although von Neumann only viewed this particular innovation as one aspect of his theory of automata. The famous "First Draft" paper also dealt with neurons and biological metaphors of computation, although this aspect of computer design was not pursued with the same enthusiasm by his followers.

For von Neumann, computers were just one stage in the evolution of automatic machinery, a term he used to describe all the artifacts of the industrial revolution. Radar, television, mechanical, and electrical computing machines were all just species of automata, whose properties and behavior could be described and analyzed with a general theory of automata. Von Neumann sought to build his theory by studying both man-made and biological systems, including living creatures, to derive his definition of automata. Nature, he argued, had come up with superb automatic machines. The reproductive mechanisms of individual cells and the nervous systems of higher animals represented important object lessons in how to go about the task of building man-made automata.

At the time, von Neumann's obsession with biology and biological metaphors seemed at odds with the task of developing computing machinery, and other innovators did not share this particular obsession. The subtle and complex processes going on in the body might make a fascinating subject for study, but biology did not seem to furnish many concrete clues for technologists. On the other hand, the success of the Eniac and its successors may have blinded the computer industry to some of the deficiencies of this basic design.

The von Neumann architecture was compact and efficient, and allowed the same machine to be set up for a wide variety of computations. Von Neumann himself thought this common repository of instructions (programs) and numbers (data) was a good model of the flexibility of the mind. But in this area, von Neumann missed the mark widely. A common repository for instructions and data leads to the von Neumann bottleneck, since the contents of memory are examined only one piece at a time. In contrast, the brain consists of billions of autonomous neurons, all of which are active simultaneously.

Modern neural research has determined that, with only a few exceptions, neurons respond to the frequency of pulses rather than to the number of some digital code. The efficiency of the brain derived from the high degree of interconnectivity, rather than from the performance of individual units. The von Neumann blueprint has taken a completely different approach. While the individual electronic components of a von Neumann machine are a million times faster and far more reliable than neurons, the interconnectivity is very low. Electronic logic gates can tolerate only a few inputs and outputs before they bog down.

The simplification of one-step-at-a-time operation helped the fledgling computer era focus on building up what von Neumann called the organs of computation. Processors, printers, memory devices and the like were all quickly developed, but were all based on serial, nonsimultaneous operation. The absence of parallel operations is the Achilles heel of digital computation.

Microchip Perfect for Digital

The digital microchip has been found to be the perfect technology to embody in a von Neumann architecture computer the ideas of Boole and Turing. The discoveries that led to microchips were based on special electronic effects that occur in many solids. After much speculation, the nature of those effects was finally explained by the theory of transistor effects discovered at AT&T's Bell Laboratories in 1948. Transistor methods produced tiny electronic components that were rugged and consumed very little electricity compared to the electronics of the time, vacuum tubes. Manufacturers were quick to realized that small, cheap, and rugged consumer products could be built with them, and, by using vast numbers of them, their inherent inaccuracies can be overcome with clever engineering.

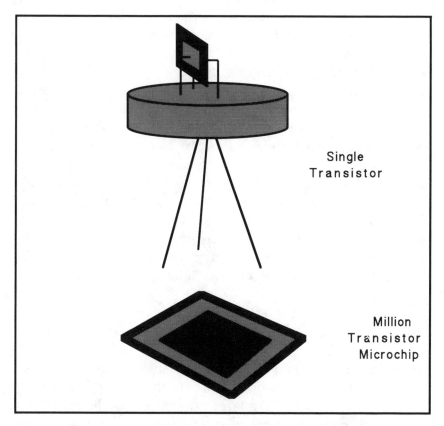

Single
Transistor

Million
Transistor
Microchip

Transistors. Single transistors built in the 1950s and 1960s are now much bulkier than million transistor microchips. In the future, microchip densities will increase about an order of magnitude more, but not indefinitely since atomic limitations are quickly approaching.

More than anything else, computer designers seized on the transistor for space and power-saving opportunities. But they soon realized that transistors' inherent inaccuracies were irrelevant for digital computers which need only to distinguish between two states, 0 and 1. Even the sloppiest circuitry can tell a 1 from a 0.

The rival approach, called analog computing, could not cope with this kind of variation. An analog computer ran the same sort of formal programs as a digital computer, but they depended upon precise voltage levels to represent numbers, so the less accurate the components, the less useful the computer itself. Von Neumann foresaw that the accuracy problem would condemn analog computers. Increasing the accuracy of an analog machine requires advances in technical expertise and increasingly better control of material processes.

But digital machines can be made more accurate simply by adding more components. The progression from 4- to 8- to 16- to 32-bit microprocessors shows this principle in action. The same basic manufactured components are placed on each new microprocessor chip, but the size of numbers that can be stored and shifted around the chip doubles each time. The components themselves do not have to be more accurate. Once a standard level of accuracy has been established, the problem of extending the precision of a digital computer is simply a matter of making more components. Though transistors were ill adapted to analog computing, they were perfect for digital.

Origins of the Microchip

The microchip combined a new innovation in electronics, the tiny transistor, with earlier ideas from lithography used with the printing press. By making large templates and then shrinking them with photolithography, manufacturers could place hundreds of transistors on the same microchip. The critical electronic effects that make the transistor possible are introduced and controlled by implanting impurities in the silicon crystal from which the chip is made. These impurities diffuse into the surface of the chip from gasses containing them, which flow over the chip. Exactly where the impurities end up can be controlled by painting a resistive coating on the top of the chip and then etching away the coating wherever a specific impurity is needed. This basic process can be repeated many times to introduce different kinds of impurities and build up a complex pattern of electronic devices in a shallow layer at the surface of a silicon chip. Many transistors could be built with the same amount of material and manufacturing effort it previously took to build a single transistor. This trend toward increasing complexity for a nominal cost gave digital system designers a crucial edge.

The sharply falling prices and steeply rising performance curves of computer systems are a direct result of the ability to crowd more and more complex functions onto the same sized microchip. Computer designers are still struggling to catch up with this explosion of computational power while software developers are, in turn, struggling to make use of the new computer hardware.

These advanced microchip manufacturing techniques boosted digital computers into the dominance they enjoy today. Digital precision in numerical calculations is measured simply by the number of bits (1s and 0s) that are available to represent numbers. By putting more and more bits onto chips and then linking more and more chips together, an arbitrary amount of precision can be built into a computer system. The superior precision of the digital approach continues today. Chips with as many as four million transistors have been demonstrated at several major electronics companies.

However, the capability of putting many transistors on a single chip does not automatically produce a computer. Even at today's densities, only parts of a functioning computer can be put on a single chip. The chips must be organized into groups on boards and the boards connected together in boxes. Often, mundane physical problems like heat buildup interfere with an otherwise perfect logical scheme, rendering a design useless.

There is also a geometric multiplying effect in the difficulty of achieving higher and higher levels of performance. One can either make the devices run faster to do more in the same amount of time, or add more chips to handle more information with one operation. Each approach takes its toll. Faster speeds mean more heat buildup, and adding more chips aggravates the problem of linking them together.

These fundamental problems do not go away with improved semiconductor fabrication methods. The leading-edge computers of today are more than ever preoccupied with cooling systems and wiring schemes. High-speed semiconductors have also compounded problems with other aspects of computer design. These days electrical events happen so fast on chips that the time to send signals between them begins to nullify that speed. A bit in a wire travels only one inch in the time it takes a state-of-the-art transistor to switch from 0 to 1.

The barriers inherent in any physical device used to represent information quickly become obvious in current-day computer design projects. The fundamental conceptual problems are becoming more and more difficult to define. What problems are most important to solve? How can they be efficiently represented in a machine?

Digital Computers Today

The early work on designing and building computers was done without regard to cost, ease-of-use or space and power limitations. Soon, however, commercial enterprises began to recognize the value of solving those problems. A general computational device could enhance business operations if it could be housed in a cabinet and plugged into normal power outlets.

For several reasons, business was a good market for selling computers. Compared to the kind of calculations required in the scientific and engineering fields where the computer was created, business computations were relatively simple. The business community is also widespread and controls a large amount of money, which they are willing to spend to get a competitive

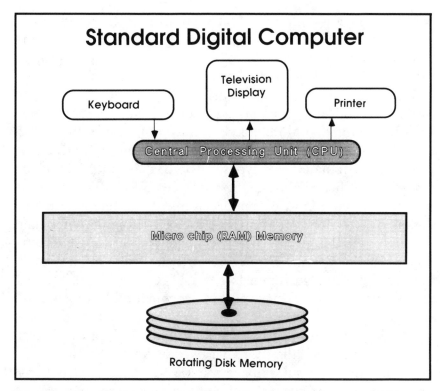

Standard Digital Computer

Keyboard

Television Display

Printer

Central Processing Unit (CPU)

Micro chip (RAM) Memory

Rotating Disk Memory

Digital Computer. The standard digital computer improves upon von Neumann's original design by extending the single-memory concept with rotating disks that can hold various different programs of instructions and data. They are loaded into RAM memories on demand.

edge. The peripheral devices to print and store information, still a major stumbling block in computer development, are simpler in the office environment as well.

In the office, keyboards and printers are the main input and output (I/O) devices, and these could be easily adapted from the electronic typewriter. Other office equipment has also been adapted as I/O devices such as numeric keypads derived from the adding machine and automatic plotters derived from manual drafting equipment.

The business-oriented, mainframe computer became the bread and butter of the emerging computer industry. It was based entirely on digital integrated circuits which began to appear en masse from burgeoning manufacturing companies. Industrial computer designers were given at cheaper and cheaper prices, an increasingly varied array of chips with which to implement their ideas.

Whatever advantage could be gained from alternative approaches to the digital method began to disappear in this flood of digital microchips and technology. The ability of digital microchips to simulate other types of approaches nullified the advantages of other methods. One might be able to get an answer faster with some kind of analog circuit, for example, but the digital environment could provide a block of digital chips that would imitate this circuit closely enough to make its use uneconomic. Digital designs quickly became the tried and accepted method by electronic engineers.

IBM put this mimicking aspect of the computer to good use in its design strategy. A basic processor was built that had the ability to mimic efficiently a whole product line of machines. The basic innovation they used has become known as microcoding. Normally, computers have a large variety of instructions that are kept in various types of memory as required. For example, a small list of frequently used instructions might be kept in a special memory chip closely connected to the main processor. In microcoding, this strategy is taken to its limit. A very small set of operations are distilled from the larger, standard instruction set that the computer accepts. Each larger instruction can then be mimicked with a small sequence of these more basic, microcoded operations. The microcode is then placed in a small, high-speed memory so the central processor can run sequences of these instructions rapidly. In this way, the same machine can be modified by programmers familiar with the microcode so that it will accept different sets of instructions. Microcode allowed IBM to package the same piece of hardware that could be mass produced, and make it look like an entirely different machine to different users.

Software was also enlisted in the drive to make computers more flexible and useful. The language of the computer could be made to resemble English more closely by creating high-level computer languages. While these languages might still look obscure and full of technical gibberish to the uninitiated, they were a vast improvement over the coding systems they replaced. And the computer itself was enlisted for the job of translating these more natural computer languages into the language of the computer itself, strings of 0s and 1s.

The increasing power of the underlying hardware has continued to allow ever-higher software entities to be more flexible and useful to the humans who ultimately have to instruct the computer to accomplish their work.

The availability of cheap digital functions also inspired computer makers to bring out smaller versions that were cheaper than the mainframe. Digital Equipment Corp. pioneered this strategy by introducing the minicomputer. These smaller, cheaper machines found their way into more varied environments than just business offices. Companies that did not need or could not afford a mainframe would buy minicomputers for specific tasks. An engineering office, for example, might buy one to aid its designers in engineering calculations and design work. Thus, the minicomputer began opening up the more difficult technical and scientific markets.

The invention of the microprocessor—a computer on a single microchip—speeded the synergy generated by cheaper computing power and more varied applications. The microprocessor represented the first attempt to place an entire functioning unit of the computer on a single chip. The idea originated in an attempt to do for calculators what IBM had done for large computers, that is, build one piece of hardware that could be reprogrammed for a whole product line.

The microprocessor was first viewed as a cheap way of making peripheral devices in the office and factory more amenable to computer control. By adding a microprocessor to a peripheral, the machine would be able to converse with a larger computer in its own language.

However, innovators quickly began looking at the microprocessor as a way of further miniaturizing the computer itself. The

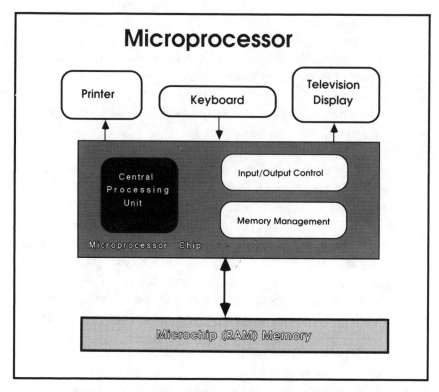

Microprocessor. The modern microprocessor, such as those used in personal computers and simple automata such as automatic bank tellers, combine a central-processing unit, input and output control circuitry, and memory addressing functions on a single silicon microchip.

design of early microprocessors was based on the minicomputer that carved out a more general market for computing machinery. Engineers who came into contact with the early microprocessors were intrigued by the idea of a complete system on a single, very inexpensive chip. What used to cost millions could now be bought by anyone for $50.

Naturally, other aspects of a computer needed to be perfected. Memory storage, for example, has always proved to be a special irritation for computer designers. Semiconductors elegantly solved the problem of building high-speed computational devices, but these processors must get numbers from somewhere and then after processing them, store them somewhere else.

The process of fetching and storing information turned out to be inherently slower than the computational processes themselves. The perfect solution would be to store all relevant information on the same chip as the computational circuitry, but this solution is not possible with today's technology.

Semiconductor technology has never fully solved the information storage problem, although it continues to yield incrementally better solutions. The first information storage devices that departed from vacuum tubes were called magnetic core memories. These used small bits of soft iron to represent a bit. The magnetic orientation of the iron could be reversed by sending a current through a wire on which the piece of iron was mounted. This same system would also allow the magnetic orientation to be sensed electronically. Because magnetic fields are permanent when left to themselves, this system allowed a means of storing and remembering bits. The 1s could be represented by one magnetic orientation, the 0s by the opposite orientation.

Transistors on integrated circuits were also enlisted in representing information. It is possible to build a memory storage device with a regular array of digital gates. These devices became known as RAMs, for *random access memory*. Because a computer organizes its memory just like street addresses in a city, the computational unit of the computer can calculate an address and send out a request to its memory for the information stored there. RAMs allow any location to be addressed, read from, or written to as easily as any other. The name is somewhat misleading, though, since almost all memory storage devices are built to allow access at any random memory location.

Microchip memory technology has been helpful in modern computer design, but it has not entirely solved the data storage problem. RAMs allow computer designers to temporarily store and retrieve small amounts of information. This process speeds up the computation since the retrieval of information from slow mechanical memories, such as magnetic cores, magnetic tapes, or disks, involves delays much longer than the processing time. If every step in a calculation required using magnetic memories, the advantage of high-speed microprocessors would be entirely nullified.

Modern computer architectures have reached the fundamental physical speed limits of technology. The largest computers in the world, called appropriately supercomputers must use large numbers of the fastest memory chips in order to profit from their high processor speeds. A leading supercomputer maker, Cray Research Inc., found that by simply replacing their dynamic RAM chips with faster static RAMs, they could triple their system performance. The next machine from Cray will abandon silicon microchips altogether in favor of a newer type of fast semiconductor made from a compound of gallium and arsenic.

Another limitation, the time delay of electric signals moving in the wires between chips and circuit boards, makes it necessary to pack the microchips more densely. As a result, the heat they generate threatens to melt the whole processor. Cooling systems necessary to prevent meltdowns are thus responsible for a major portion of the high cost of supercomputers.

To overcome the fundamental physical limits now being confronted, the foremost computer architects are designing so-called parallel processors. These processors harness multitudes of single von Neumann processors simultaneously to form supercomputers. Researchers, however, are quickly discovering that the problems of coordinating the activities of many processors simultaneously is even more difficult than building a smaller faster one.

The computer revolution is running up against fundamental physical limits. Without new strategies, conventional von Neumann architectures, even those harnessing many processors simultaneously, simply can not cope with the increasing complexity of systems.

All Is Not Lost

Still, all is not lost, because the brain itself offers a model for harnessing many processors simultaneously. Studies of the electrical behavior of the individual nerve cells in the brain show that they perform a variety of useful operations. Some of these operations are equivalent to digital Boolean computations, but others use radically new methods.

A theory explaining all the operations that neurons perform has not been found. The 100 billion neurons in the brain all perform operations simultaneously, and exactly what they communicate to one another is still subject to debate.

However, while no one has completely unraveled the operational structure of the brain, the scale of its power is precisely what is needed to advance beyond conventional computers. A square centimeter of the brain's cortex, or outer layer, has a million neurons with over one billion interconnecting fibers, called dendrites. These fibers are far smaller in diameter than the interconnection wires within state-of-the-art microchips, and they interconnect the neurons in three dimensions rather than two. An increasing amount of overall structure is being deciphered, but the scale of the problem has made it difficult for brain researchers to theorize about this enormous tangle of interconnections.

In computers, which are currently man's only models of such complexity, the circuits are carefully laid out according to logical plans, and all electrical events are carefully timed and controlled. A master clock sends timing signals to every device in the circuit to ensure that computation proceeds along its carefully predestined course. No such clock or determinant organization can be found in the apparently random firing of neurons. Yet people can still resolve two-dimensional images and interpret them as three-dimensional scenes, accomplish precise motor operations such as walking on only two legs while contemplating such highly abstract concepts as a bank balance. With all their high speed and refined organization, computers are still far from doing any one of these tasks well, let alone all of them at the same time.

It is immediately evident even to a novice that computers and minds belong to two different categories. One researcher reduced this difference to numbers: It would take millions of today's computers to reproduce the operations of the mind, and it would equally take millions of minds to do the kind of high-speed calculations routine to computers. They are fundamentally different.

Others use the concept of psychological relevance to express this gap. When computers depart from the intended plan of calculation, they become incomprehensible. However, when people make mistakes, they generally have some accurate intuitions about where the problem is.

Computer researchers never abandoned the attempt to build systems that behave like the brain. The blanket term *artificial intelligence* (AI) has been applied to attempts of this kind. AI research has produced digital computer systems that seem to reason as people do and are easier for human operators to use. The approach, called *expert systems,* has even hit the commercial computer world as an alternative to advice from human experts. This turn of events was a surprise to many commercial computer makers since AI research was always regarded as too esoteric to have any useful applications.

Still, this mimicking of intelligence is not what the AI community has traditionally sought. One of the crucial differences between human thinking and machine computation is what one AI researcher calls the spurious precision of the digital computer.

Computers are excellent at finding the answer to a problem and finding it to great degrees of accuracy. Humans, on the other hand, tend to get bored with calculations that run too long. The fundamental and practical reason for this boredom is that *accuracy can actually impede a system's ability to control a process.* In reacting to live situations—such as controlling some machine in a factory—computers will often go beyond the required precision and waste time, decreasing their efficiency. A related problem occurs when a calculation is already very close to the exact value required. Since the computer has no way of judging the difference between close and very close, in some situations, it will mindlessly keep computing closer and closer values without realizing that the value it had originally was good enough.

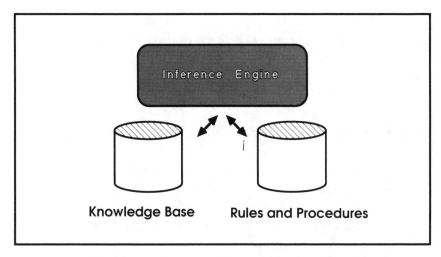

Expert System. So-called "expert systems" achieve their measure of artificial intelligence (AI) by reasoning according to the algorithms in an "inference engine" based on facts from a dynamic knowledge base according to a set of rules and procedures.

This problem was belatedly recognized by digital system designers and partially remedied by introducing a new logical system. Called *fuzzy logic*, this system introduces more alternatives than the simple *yes* and *no* of Boolean logic. Instead of always dealing in absolute yes or no, true or false terms, fuzzy logic has a range of values that represent degrees of truth. For example, people would consider someone who is six-feet tall tall, while someone who is five-feet tall would be described as short, but what about someone who is five-feet-eleven-inches? Definitely not short, but not as tall as a six foot person. Although there are definitely tall and short people in a given sample of the population, there is no definite height where tall suddenly becomes short.

With fuzzy logic, the concept tall can be assigned a continuous range of values, degrees of set membership, in which taller than means having a higher value. Computer systems can then be made to compare these set membership values. Fuzzy logic, then, enables a computer to come up with more reasonable answers, the kind that humans might respond with, rather than the most accurate answer. The price of this more realistic logic system, however, is paid in the form of higher processing demands.

Learning Rather Than Programming

The major difference between computers and humans is that computers are programmed, whereas humans learn. Although the expert systems can take the knowledge acquired by a human expert and automate the reasoning process, they still cannot learn anything new on their own.

Human relationships are full of ambiguous situations. We regard the police as a positive institution that protects us from wrongdoers, but we also break laws that make us subject to arrest by the same organization. In a repressive society, basic values that we hold to be good and true could become a fundamental threat to our well-being.

We might be able to reduce considerably the psychological stress of modern life if we had a machine that could automatically generate the one true answer to any social dilemma. Since such a machine will never be built, we must grow up with our own mental circuitry and its ability to learn, perhaps slowly and painfully, from its mistakes and miscalculations. Learning seems to require the ability to consider logically contradictory propositions and weigh their relative merits in the light of new experience, but logical systems on computers cannot even take the first step. Neither Boole nor anyone else has come up with a logical calculus that can simultaneously model mutually contradictory circumstances.

For researchers trying to break through the barrier facing current computer architectures, the fuzzy logic seems a long route to a nearby goal. It advocates building a highly precise machine whose enormous calculating power can emulate imprecise thinking. Expert systems, on the other hand, are an attempt to graft symbolic reasoning onto machinery that continuously weighs the different sides to each question separately. But the brain, with its lack of logical organization and control, weighs mutually contradictory circumstances simultaneously. What's more, it appears an element of chaos is necessary to the internally self-contradictory nature of thought.

Extensive experience with one of von Neumann's suggestions, the stored program digital computer, has thus turned up more reasons for taking his full original program more seriously. It turns out that there is a lot more to building computers than simply numbers, precision, and blinding speed.

Von Neumann not only foresaw that digital techniques would dominate, he also cautioned that the digital approach would force computer theory into the least developed area of mathematical theory, discrete mathematics. The most developed area of mathematical theory uses continuous variables rather than discrete, on-off states. Von Neumann suggested that probability theory might be the bridge between the two, and the theory of fuzzy logic seems to be one attempt to build this bridge.

The Austrian physicist Ludwig Boltzmann made a similar attempt to unite discrete and continuous realms. In the late nineteenth century, Boltzmann tried to build a bridge between the microscopic world of atoms and the everyday world of continuous, indivisible substances. Boltzmann's ultimate hope was to find some way of tracing the behavior of complex phenomena back to the simple laws of interacting particles. He failed in this grand program, but even his failure was a brilliant success in its own way. His theory of statistical mechanics came out of this failed effort and has provided scientists with a basic language for thinking about large, complex systems.

Von Neumann suggested that an adequate theory of automata would complete this program of Boltzmann's. Such a theory would have to explain how chaotically interacting particles could lead to coherent, organized systems. It is clear that organized systems arise in this way in biology, but the overall process remains a mystery. The nature of the brain, which is composed of billions of independently acting cells, nevertheless can think feel, and sometimes even compute.

At a symposium held in Pasadena in 1948, John von Neumann summarized his thought on the future of computer technology. One of the members of the audience was Warren McCulloch, then the world's only neural network researcher. In the early 1940s, McCulloch and a co-researcher, Walter Pitts, had published papers on their efforts to model neurons with electronic components. These models mimicked the properties of neurons as they were then known. McCulloch-and-Pitts neurons (as they came to be called) responded to input with an all or nothing output.

In itself, this work would not have created a sensation in scientific circles, but McCulloch and Pitts went farther in their theoretical assessment of the models. They derived some general properties of networks of such devices. Although researchers had been studying neurons for centuries, no one had a clue where to begin unraveling the dense interconnecting network of neurons in the brain. McCulloch and Pitts provided the first clue.

Their main point about neural networks was supported by von Neumann in his 1948 Pasadena lecture, in which he predicted that any behavior that can be described in language or any other notation can be produced by a suitably connected network of McCulloch-and-Pitts neurons. Von Neumann included the behavior of the ideal computer—a Turing machine—as a special case of this theorem, pointing out that other types of behavior are difficult or impossible for computers.

It would be fairly easy, von Neumann reasoned, to connect some McCulloch-and-Pitts neurons to imitate a Turing Machine. But what about building a network that performed the everyday tasks of cognition, such as recognizing triangles and squares? In answer, von Neumann pointed out a curious aspect of McCulloch and Pitts' network theorem. He claimed that the full description of human object-recognition abilities might turn out to be more complex than the network of neurons in the brain that performs it.

For centuries, man has been able to understand his machines by breaking them down into simple parts with specific functions. The wet ware in the brain, many have thought, could eventually be simply described with a few basic terms. However, von Neumann believed that humans, considered as automata, were fundamentally different from machines. He suspected that any attempt to describe in simple terms something as complex as the brain would inevitably become entangled in endless complications. Such complex automata, as opposed to manmade devices, might have the property that they are already their own simplest description.

This conclusion implies that the network structure of the brain is itself the best description of the brain and that any attempt to break it down into simpler machines, such as AI agents, is doomed to fail. Such a conclusion also has serious implications for anyone attempting to build machines that mimic the brain. People construct machines by piecing together simple parts with clearly defined purposes. All the parts in a car, for instance, are inherently simpler than the car itself, as are the drawings that define the car. How would people go about building one of von Neumann's complex automata if the description were more complex than the machine? According to this analysis, one couldn't start with designs and parts.

How does nature do it? The answer is at first simple: self-reproduction. Complex automata are able to make perfect copies of themselves. Nature also never starts over from scratch; its creativity is confined to modifying and adapting previous constructions. Adaptation, mutation, and reproduction seem to be the tools that natural processes use to create complex automata. Von Neumann pointed out that the evolutionary process seems to imply a logical contradiction in that simpler machines produce more complicated machines. However, he gave a proof that the process is, in fact, rigorously logical, with no contradiction involved, by describing in precise detail an automaton that could reproduce itself.

That first result of his early theory of automata suggested that a theory explaining biological organization was possible, and that it might yield a blueprint for manmade automata—cognizers. The current crisis in the computer industry demonstrates that such a comprehensive theory is still badly needed.

Cognizers

Von Neumann died in the late 1950s while still developing his comprehensive scheme for the design of automata. He expected intelligent, cognizant machinery to be the next great phase in the industrial revolution.

The synthesis of biology, physics, and technology that he hoped for may finally be here. Once again, his problem was that contemporary technology hid essential clues. Since then, researchers have continued to study neurons, attempting to unravel their language. Biology, too, has undergone a fundamental revolution. The discovery of the DNA molecule and the machinery of the cell has shown that living things are in fact assembled from myriads of tiny self-replicating machines. The cell creates a living organism by processing the information written in a code stored in a DNA molecule, a process which bears an uncanny resemblance to Turing's original conception of a computing machine. Cognizers could merge the two to create machines that are truly, as opposed to artificially, intelligent.

2

The Secret of Life

Learning from Frankenstein's Mistakes

The Italian scientist Luigi Galvani dazzled the imagination of man when he discovered that dead frogs' legs would respond to electric currents as if they were alive. That discovery began a frenzy of scientific research and popular literature fascinated with the idea that electricity had some fundamental relation to the mystery of life.

Over the years, an understanding of the electrochemical properties of the brain has grown steadily. Repeatedly, the technology of the time has led to bold new ideas. Now, the technology of our times, electronic microchips, is helping to build synthetic nervous systems—cognizers.

From Galvani's manuscripts in the 1700s to Andy Warhol's twentieth-century rendition of *Frankenstein*, man continues to wonder if electricity somehow creates life. The most notable result of this activity is the modern computer itself, which was inspired by John von Neumann's simple models of nerve cells.

Throughout history, immature research methods have repeatedly thwarted an understanding of the mysteries of the brain. Even though a medical understanding of the brain's physiological needs and maintenance has grown steadily, and successful spin-offs like the digital computer have been of great utility, a conceptual understanding of how the nervous system causes us to be self-aware and enables us to think in terms of objects and ideas has not been forthcoming. However, modern scientists, merging biology with electronic microchips, have finally started to discover how electrochemical activity holds the secret of sentient life. Life is not some mysterious force; rather it is a subtle and complex pattern of electrical activity in a chemical medium. From brain to spinal cord to the countless nerve endings in the skin, the cooperative actions of nerve cells cause the realm of thought to arise. A detailed understanding of that pattern of activity is the key to cognizing.

The Incredible Brain

Even in its most primitive state, animate matter is strikingly different from inanimate. For the first time in recorded history, the musing of theorists has combined with experimental observation to filter the essence of this difference from the endless complexities of chemistry. A new movement, referred to as *nonlinear science*, seeks to explain how the mechanisms of the cell can appear to create spontaneously the diversity of life.

The first confirmation of the spontaneous-generation-of-life hypothesis came from an experiment performed in the early 1960s. This experiment was a laboratory demonstration of how lightning striking a primordial sea could produce the building blocks of living proteins. A mixture of the kind of chemicals that existed in the atmosphere and sea of primordial Earth was prepared. Electric discharges were then used to energize chemical reactions. Surprisingly, a bewildering array of amino acids spontaneously appeared after this electrical treatment. Proteins, which are the structural elements of the body, are simple chains of these amino acids, different proteins consisting of different sequences of amino acids, just as different words are different sequences of the same 26 letters.

The experiment suggested that the primordial seas were a rich chemical laboratory in which some kind of evolutionary mechanism or mechanisms were at work. Any number of natural repositories of chemical reactions could have provided the site for evolutionary mechanisms. The crowning achievement of this protean chemical evolution was the individual cell, which turns out to be a very complex mechanism. Researchers now know that cells are self-contained machines with a built-in set of directives that guide them. They have the remarkable ability to build identical copies of themselves, which then wander off fulfilling the same objectives as the original. The copies then produce copies, and the resulting explosion is called growth. Perhaps all earthly living organisms can be traced back to the first such cell which evolved from the proteins created by natural selection among a sea of amino acids.

But growth processes are not a simple chaotic profusion of identical cells. The cells change as they reproduce and become specialized to fulfill functions required by the organism they are building. All the different parts of the body are built from cells that, on the inside, are exactly the same. These cells specialize only as they grow to perform the function of muscle, gland, or neuron. While little is known about the means that individual cells use to determine when and into what to specialize, researchers now know that neurons, with their unique ability to link electrically with thousands of their neighbors, are just another specialization of the original cell. Still, rigorous mathematical equations that model this activity have not been forthcoming.

Though estimates vary, humans are born with as many as 100 billion neurons, most of which reside in the brain. The incredibly complex patterns of activity that resonate among those independent units define cognition. Even though some neurons are replaced when they die, on the whole, people start with a maximum number that can only diminish over time. As people grow older, they must cram more and more experience into the complex patterns of activity of a shrinking mass of neurons.

There are two problems with studying all these neurons: their

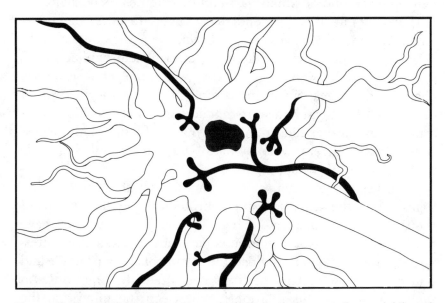

Nerve Cell and Dendrites. A neuron has a single axon (lower right) and thousands of dendrites trailing away from it that gather information from other neurons' axons (in black). The patterns among these connections determine the characteristics of the cognition.

tiny size and their large number of interconnections. Neurons are often less than 100 microns (millionth of a meter) in diameter and have as many as 10,000 connecting wires, some as small as one micron in diameter. The so-called nerves, such as those in and fanning out from the spinal cord, are actually bundles of fibers, each one of which is ultimately a part of a single neuron. A single primary fiber, called the *axon*, emerges from a neuron to pass information on to other neurons. For sensory neurons in the body, the axons serve to pass information to the brain. For neurons in the brain, axons pass information out to muscles or up to higher processing levels. Conduits to the brain from sense organs and back from the brain to the muscles, nerves actually consist of as many as 100,000 fibers or axons.

Besides the axon, a neuron has thousands of other branches, called *dendrites*, that branch off from the main body of the neuron and from the axon. Neurons use the dendrites to gather information. Thousands of dendrites can be attached to a single neuron, each one of which partially determines its behavior.

The points at which a dendrite connects to other dendrites and axons are called *synapses*. The synapse is the contact point between two neurons. Unlike a direct electrical connection, a synapse is a microscopic gap across which one neuron passes chemical messages, of varying complexity, to another neuron. A multitude of natural and some not so natural chemicals in that synaptic gap either aid or inhibit synaptic firing. Many drugs, such as tranquilizers, work by modifying the natural chemicals that reside in the synaptic gap.

The revelation that neurons communicate with chemical messages across the synaptic gap has brought the critical minds of thousands of researchers to bear on the problem. They have found that thoughts and emotions have direct physical manifestations among the neurons and the chemicals they produce and that changes among the neurons can affect the emotions. An understanding of this relationship between the mind and the body is not only helping to build synthetic minds (cognizers), but is also coming to show how to control the immune system with the mind.

The History of Neural Research

Historically, neural research has always been dependent on the technology used to investigate it. From ancient times till now, new technological developments have had to precede any new understanding of neurons. Though the relationship between the mind and body was the beginning point for brain researchers, it has only recently come to be understood explicitly.

From ancient times, philosophers have allowed a priori ideas to hamper genuine progress. Starting in 400 B.C., the Greek philosopher Plato taught that a perfect heaven rained down ethereal spirits that entered and vitalized the body. These spirits bestowed the perfection of heaven on mortal man by entering the body through its various orifices. Plato concluded from this analysis that the brain must concentrate these spirits in the production of semen.

His reasoning was that semen obviously transferred the soul of the male into the female, causing pregnancy. Such perfection in nature, Plato reasoned, could only be the result of some perfect organ in the body. Since the brain resides inside the relatively perfect sphere of the cranium, then it must be the producer of semen. Plato's student Aristotle improved on this line of reasoning very little, concluding that the heart must be the residence of the soul while the brain merely cooled the blood.

Solid research into the makeup of the human nervous system was not started till 130 A.D., when the Roman Claudius Galenus (Galen) had the opportunity to ponder empirical evidence rather than philosophical speculation. Galen embarked on a medical career because his father, an architect, had a sleeping vision that the God of Medicine (Aesculapius) wanted Galen to be a doctor. This vision must have been true because Galen's medical prowess led him to the courts of Emperor Marcus Aurelius, where he distinguished himself by discovering the difference between motor and sensory nerves.

From his work with fallen gladiators, Galen discovered that it was possible to sustain damage to the sensory nerves without affecting the motor nerves. Gladiators with damaged spinal cords often regained motor control but not feeling in specific limbs. That observation led Galen to speculate on the composition and function of nerves. Galen's pioneering work laid a foundation that was not improved upon until the seventeenth century when new technology, the microscope, made it possible to refine his notions.

Galen, brilliant as he was, could not have discovered the true functioning of nerves with the technology of his time. The most advanced technology available was an understanding of fluid flow in Roman aqueducts. Accordingly, Galen taught that the nerves were hollow tubes, like the blood vessels, through which an infinitely finer substance flowed.

Galen's analysis, modeled on Plato's, was that food entered the stomach, was digested, and passed on to the liver where it was transformed into a substance called *animal spirits*. The animal spirits were then sent on to the heart where they were transformed into the *vital spirits* that fortified the body. Vital spirits were carried in the blood to the brain where they were

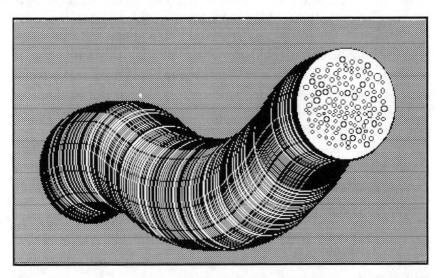

Nerve Fibers. The inside of the macroscopic nerve fibers visible to physicians is filled with thousands of microscopic individual axons. Some axons are taking sensory information up to the brain, some are taking motor information from the brain down to the muscles.

transformed into an even finer substance that flowed into the nerves themselves.

Galen's teachings remained unchanged through the seventeenth century when the great rational philosopher René Descartes elaborated on but did not contradict them. Descartes added the idea that the soul resides in the brain—specifically in the pituitary gland. Shortly after the microscope was invented in 1660, several researchers discovered simultaneously that nerves were not hollow at all but filled with a spongy substance. Nevertheless, Galen's theory persisted for lack of a better explanation.

For the next 150 years, scientists speculated wildly trying to come up with a competing theory that made as much sense as Galen's. Even Isaac Newton examined the matter and suggested that man's nerves are like harps which transmit vibrations to the body through an infinitely fine *ether* inside the nerves.

As microscope technology advanced, however, it became evident that the infinitely fine ether was not so infinitesimal, but was in fact electrochemical. Henry Cavendish first demonstrated this characteristic in the late 1700s when he showed, by conducting blindfold tests, that the shocks from eel-like fish called *torpedoes* could not be distinguished from static electricity shocks. Cavendish, however, did not draw the conclusion that the nerve force was electrical. That distinction belongs to Luigi Galvani who in 1791 showed not just that electricity could be produced by the body, but that electricity was actually a force inside nerves.

Galvani's Gift to Man

By demonstrating how frogs' legs responded to static electricity, Galvani showed conclusively that electricity could control motor nerves. Benjamin Franklin's new findings about static electricity, and his invention of the Leyden jar for holding it, gave Galvani the impetus to do his experiments.

In his most famous experiment, Galvani used static electricity stored in a Leyden jar during a storm to stimulate the severed legs of frogs. His jumping frogs' legs demonstrated not only that nerves used electricity to work, but also that electrical energy could be stored in the body. Even though he misinterpreted the mechanism of storage, leaving it to Alessandro Volta to reveal how a battery works (neurons and their surrounding bodily fluids form tiny batteries), Galvani ended centuries of philosophical speculation about the origin and workings of animal spirits. He also opened the door to the science of electrophysiology— the study of the electrical functions of living organisms. He found that the life-force was stored in the fluids that make up the bulk of the body's weight much as electricity is stored in a battery. The individual neurons act as the poles of internal batteries charged by positive and negative ions synthesized from ordinary table salt.

Though Galvani's experiments showed electricity to be the nerve's force, again the technology of the time could not accurately measure the feeble electrical currents produced by chemical reactions in nerves. In 1820, however, an instrument was

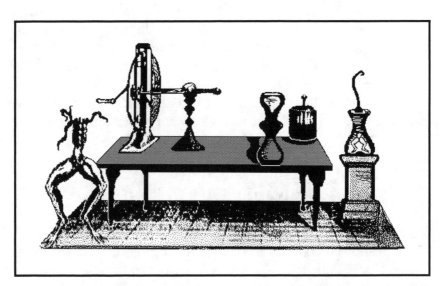

Galvani's Laboratory. This rendering of Luigi Galvani's laboratory, from his 1791 text, shows how electricity from an electrostatic generator was stored in a bell jar and used to stimulate frogs' legs. He discovered that the nerve cells act like the poles of tiny batteries.

invented that was sensitive enough to measure electrical potential in nerves. Thirty years later the German Emil Du Bois-Reymond, a student of renowned physiologist Johannes Müller, invented a set of electrodes to match the sensitivity of the galvanometer. Du Bois-Reymond's nonpolarizable electrode could be attached to living tissue without producing the noise that often spoiled earlier experimental results. To match his electrodes, Du Bois-Reymond also designed a supersensitive version of a galvanometer by using finer wire than was used in conventional galvanometers. Dubbed by Du Bois-Reymond as the *nerve galvanometer*, it allowed the first serious study of neurons to begin.

Armed with his highly sensitive galvanometer and electrodes, Du Bois-Reymond went on not only to verify that Galen's animal spirits were actually the electricity predicted by Galvani, but also to begin a careful characterization of this electricity. Du Bois-Reymond's work was confused by signals emitted from nerves he had damaged, nerves which let out a constant *current of injury*. Nevertheless, he quickly came to realize that normal neurons do not emit a constant signal, but instead emit *spikes* or

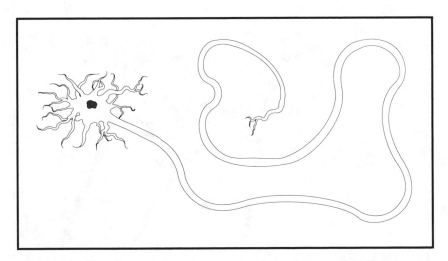

Long Axon. An individual neuron's axon can be many orders of magnitude longer than the cell body of the neuron itself. The reason that an axon must be so very long is to enable it to stimulate thousands, or in some cases tens of thousands, of other neurons.

pulses. In fact, uninjured nerves in a quiescent subject emitted no signal at all. Only when going into action (when a muscle flexed, for instance), did the healthy nerves emit signals, and even then the signal was a flurry of activity racing down the extent of the nerve, not a constant flow. By finally offering a better solution backed by facts rather than speculation, Du Bois-Reymond's detailed characterization of the nerve impulse dispelled forever Galen's animal spirits.

About the same time that Du Bois-Reymond's research began to bear fruit, other advances in the understanding of electricity were being made. Lord William Kelvin (after whom the Kelvin temperature scale was eventually named) further refined the galvanometer by attaching to it a small mirror instead of a bulky needle. By reflecting light off the small mirror, a highly accurate wall-sized scale could be used instead of the small one using the needle indicator.

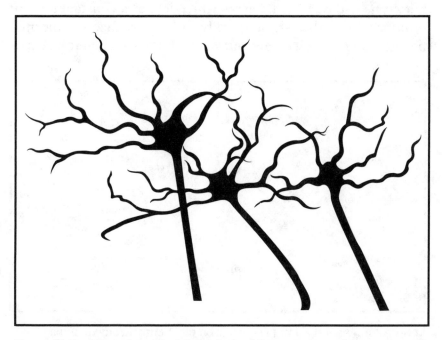

Nerve Cells. The primary building block of the nervous system, nerve cells or neurons, come in many specialized varieties. Since they do not act alone, but rather work in groups, like types can often be found together.

Using more refined tools like Lord Kelvin's reflecting galvanometer, the English physiologist Richard Canton was able to discern the difference between motor and sensory neurons, the difference Galen had hypothesized in 130 A.D. But Canton was not content to verify the results of others. By placing the electrodes from his highly sensitive reflecting galvanometer on the surface of a monkey's brain, Canton was able to detect discernible signals when sensory information, such as bright light in the monkey's eyes, was encountered. In this way, Canton not only proved Galen right, but also invented the precursor to the electroencephalogram (EEG). Canton wrote of brain waves in monkeys some 70 years before Hans Berger pronounced his discovery of what he called *alpha-waves* from human brains in 1926.

How Fast Is Nervous Energy?

A much debated topic in the middle of the nineteenth century was just how fast this newly found substance called electricity travelled. Some of the greatest minds of the era were hard at work on this problem. In the 1840s, Samuel Morse demonstrated with his telegraph that electricity traveled very fast indeed by connecting cities along the U.S. eastern seaboard. Experiments over long distances showed that electricity was faster than human reactions. The few seconds it took for confirmation messages to be returned from faraway cities could be accounted for solely by the time it took the telegraph operator to key them in. Electricity was very fast indeed.

As the telegraph wires were quickly strung up, neural researchers noticed that they branched and spread out across the countryside in a manner reminiscent of nerves. Since the telegraph clearly used electricity to send and receive messages, it was naturally surmised that nerves did too. The question was: how quickly?

The greatest scientists of the time speculated wildly, some claiming that nerves could conduct electricity as fast as 10 million miles per second. Johannes Müller, renowned in his time, taught in the 1830s that the speed of nervous energy would never be measured, being too fast for any conceivable measuring device. Perhaps it was the boldness of Müller's statement that stimulated one of his students, a physicist named Hermann von Helmholtz, to disprove that assertion. Much to his mentor's dismay, Helmholtz demonstrated that electricity, in nerves at least, traveled a mere 90 miles per hour.

Yet this pace would have made using the telegraph merely three or four times faster than taking a train! Clearly electricity traveled much more slowly in nerves than through metal wires, but why? That question became the obsession of numerous researchers armed with improved microscopes.

The solution to the slower speed of the nerve impulse began in 1838 when German botanist Matthias Schleiden and physiologist Theodor Schwann presented the cell theory of life. Almost simultaneously, Jan Purkinje pronounced that he had identified individual neurons. Purkinje, a Czechoslovakian physiologist working in Germany, described certain brain cells so accurately

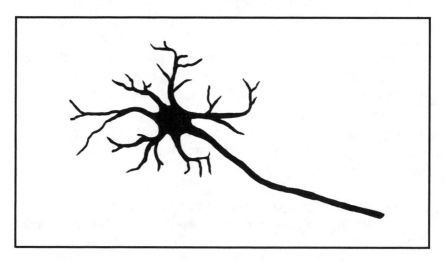

Single Neuron. Though neurons come in many varieties, they share fundamental characteristics with their brethren. For instance, they usually have many inputs (dendrites) and a single output (axon) that is many magnitudes longer than the neuron's cell body itself.

that years later those cells were named for him. However, his most profound observation was that the nerves were made up of two parts—a nerve cell's nucleus and a web of fibers. Helmholtz made the logical extension of that discovery, concluding from his own observations that these fibers were in fact extensions of the neurons themselves. Again, however, advances in technology, this time better microscopes and observation techniques, were needed to confirm Helmholtz' proposition.

Purkinje recognized that his discovery was in harmony with the theory that plants and animals are made up of individual cells rather than continuous tissues. But he did not recognize that this fact also explained the relative slowness of electricity in nerves. Instead of traveling down a single path like the telegraph, a message passes from neuron to neuron. Unfortunately neither Helmholtz nor Purkinje guessed the truth—that neurons are separate, autonomous cells.

However, from their speculation, a whole area of scientific investigation was born, dubbed *neurohistology*. One of these histologists, a German named Joseph von Gerlach, came up with an excellent stain for nerve tissue. The fine detail his stain produced led him to the discovery that one dominant fiber, now called the axon, ran from neurons to the bundles of fibers called nerves. In fact, the hair-like nerves found throughout the body were nothing more than bundles of microscopic axons, each an extension of a single neuron. Thus, Helmholtz's speculation was confirmed.

All Is One . . . or Is It?

These and other even finer observations indicated that the central nervous system was in fact one continuous, unbroken network that ran throughout the body. As more and more information flowed in, everything seemed to point to that erroneous conclusion.

When the Italian anatomist Camillo Golgi developed an especially effective stain in the 1870s, he seemed to clench the case.

Golgi observed that not only did neurons have axons, but they also had multitudes of lesser fibers attached to the axons, fibers which came to be called dendrites. Golgi surmised that the nervous system must be one continuous network with innumerable branchings. The number and complexity of the dendrites were so staggering to Golgi that he eventually abandoned the field, saying the puzzle was impossible to decipher.

This time it took a technological refinement rather than a breakthrough to unravel further the tangled web of the nervous system. Santiago Ramon Cajal, a Spanish histologist, refined Golgi's stains, and by using them to study nerve tissue in various stages of development from embryo to maturity, he was able to disprove the theory that a network of nerves is one continuous entity. Cajal's discovery of the synapse disproved once and for all Golgi's theory that the nervous system was one continuous mass. By observing that electricity always flowed from the brain to the muscles in motor nerves and from sensory sights to the brain for sensory nerves, Cajal was also able to elaborate on Canton's findings of separate motor and sensory nerves.

Waiting for Mr. Technology

The latter nineteenth and early twentieth centuries were again devoid of major breakthroughs in neural research. Not until the invention of the vacuum tube and the electron microscope could instruments be built that were precise enough to plumb the mysteries of the synaptic cleft. A single neuron develops a voltage potential of only a few thousandths of a volt, far too small for conventional passive instrumentation to detect. But with a vacuum tube, that feeble signal could be amplified thousands or even millions of times. In the early 1900s, pioneers like Edgar Adrian at the University of Pennsylvania and Joseph Erlanger and Herbert Gasser at Washington University (St. Louis), began to study and record the actions of single synapses, using vacuum tube amplifiers and cathode ray tube (CRT) oscilloscopes. The Washington University researchers finally discovered what

Helmholtz had only been able to speculate about—the reason electricity traveled so slowly in nerves. The answer was in the synaptic cleft. Electrical pulses cause chemical transmitters to be released in the synapse; these transmitters then pass a message along to the next neuron. When a neuron fires, it passes an impulse along its axon that causes the axon to exchange electrically charged ions with the fluids surrounding the cell. Those ions, however, never bridge the synaptic gap; instead, a chemical message is sent to the receiving neuron. This chemical side of a neuron explained why its operation was slower than would be expected from a purely electrical device.

When a neuron fires, little trap doors open along its axon, doors that are ordinarily held shut electrically by muscles that respond to the difference in charge between the outside and inside of the neuron. Common table salt, for instance, is broken down by the body into sodium (+) and chloride ions (−). While the salty bodily fluids are positively charged with sodium, the inside of the neuron is negatively charged with chloride, and an ion pump keeps it that way so that the trap doors stay shut. But as the neurotransmitter chemicals gradually change that potential difference, the trap door latches eventually give way and open.

When a group of these trap doors open, the inrush of ions creates a disturbance in the electrical field which causes neighboring trap doors to open. The neuron then fires, causing a wave of successive trap door openings radiating down the axon. That action stimulates the deposition of neurotransmitter chemicals on each of the thousands of neurons to which the axon is attached. The electrochemical messages can travel to that many other neurons because the axon's firing is self-perpetuating. Since the ion pump is going all the time to replenish lost ions, a neuron takes about a thousandth of a second to recharge after a successful firing.

Nearly a hundred years earlier, Du Bois-Reymond had observed the gross effects of this jerky behavior of neurons. And in the early 1900s, the German physiologist Julius Bernstein had proposed the membrane theory of nerve connections that predicted much of what has now been discovered. But it took the detailed observations of synaptic action to explain the behavior accurately. As early as 1921, the Austrian physiologist Otto Loewi found that a certain chemical, now called acetylcholine, could affect the speed at which nerves react. Not until a detailed understanding of the synapse was achieved, however, could his findings be explained.

At Washington University, Erlanger and Gasser mapped out the synapse. They found through observation of the behavior of numerous nerve types that the speed of nervous energy was also dependent upon the size of nerves. Larger diameter nerves, such as motor nerves, are able to accumulate electrical charge at the synaptic sites quickly, making for more voluminous chemical production and quicker reactions to stimuli. Larger nerves are also faster because they are encased in an insulating substance that keeps the electrical impulse from dissipating between their more sparsely placed trap doors.

Sensory nerves, on the other hand, were found to use smaller fibers that took longer to transmit messages. This difference accounts for why it takes longer to feel the burning sensation than to remove the hand from a hot stove. But it was not until 1939 that these descriptions could be explained and Bernstein's membrane theory be proven correct.

The New Zealand researcher, John Eccles, conclusively confirmed Bernstein's membrane theory with the invention of the micropipette. These tiny glass tubes were small enough to penetrate the membrane of a single synapse. The fluid inside the micropipette was then able to conduct the electrical potentials up to an oscilloscope where the actions inside and outside the membrane could be simultaneously observed.

With the verification of Bernstein's membrane theory, it was now also possible to explain Loewi's observation that chemicals like acetylcholine could affect nervous activity. Acetylcholine has since become the best known transmitter substance. Gradually it was found that a multitude of transmitter chemicals existed and that each had a certain site in the nervous system where it acted.

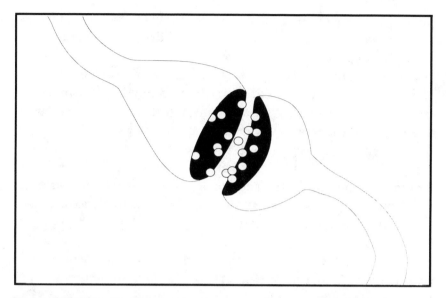

Synaptic Knob. The thousands of neurons that control bodily functions do not communicate with one another directly. Minute gaps between them—the synapse—converts electrical impulses into chemicals that pass messages alone to their neighboring neurons.

An understanding of the actions of synapses and transmitter substances as the carriers of charge was forthcoming. The combined chemical and electrical effects were linked for the first time to show that the electrical charge passed along the axon to a synapse where it released a quantity of transmitter chemical. What action was then taken depended on the specific chemical released. Some chemicals immediately caused the receiving neuron to fire, others only increased the chance of the receiving cell firing, and others actually inhibited the receiving neuron from firing.

The diversity of chemical activity in the synapse set off a rage of experimentation that produced a barrage of new drugs whose action sites were the synaptic cleft. Both LSD (1943) and the common tranquilizer (1952) were discovered during these searches, as was nerve gas, which knocks out synaptic firing altogether. Botulism was found to be caused by a toxin that prevented acetylcholine release in 1949, and in 1960, Parkinson's disease was found to be responsive to a drug that partially restored synaptic transmitter balance.

While an understanding of the mechanisms of the synaptic cleft has led medical researchers down many fruitful paths, it has led other scientists down many fruitless ones. The basic tenet that led them astray was that a better understanding of the mechanisms of consciousness required an ever closer look inside neurons. This kind of thinking was reminiscent of physicists looking for the basic building blocks of matter who found only more and more elementary particles the harder they looked. Still researchers hypothesized that in the quickly developing field of genetics, a full understanding of the brain would be found. To find those hidden inside components of consciousness, researchers took to electron microscopes, genetic splicing, and X-ray holography.

But, though an ever expanding understanding of how cells grow and maintain themselves has been achieved, a better understanding of how the organism as a whole copes with its environment remained elusive. It took a blending of concepts from mathematics, psychology, physiology, and computer science to take the next step in understanding.

Donald Hebb, a psychologist at McGill University, speculated that the axons and dendrites might form patterns among the folds of the brain. These patterns were subsequently found to be formed by the configuration of the connections among neurons. Later experiments suggested that new connections in the brain could be made almost simultaneously with new experiences. At first it was thought that individual sites in the brain contained specific pieces of information; after a continual failure to decipher the code, however, it was concluded that a deeper understanding of the microscopic workings of neurons was not the answer.

It's not something deep inside the cells themselves that explains how living beings feel and think. That domain is mainly involved with growth and genetic inheritance. The part of the nervous system that adapts to the environment is not inside but among the neurons. The connecting patterns themselves are the characteristics that represent learned responses, and ultimately the human personality. Helmholtz observed the grossest aspects of this phenomena, that thick fibers were fast and small ones were slow. But it took the catalyst of a refined twentieth-century understanding of electronics to deduce that different modes of behavior are the result of connections changed by learning. No one connection can determine behavior, but the vastly complex web of interconnected neurons all stimulating each other appears to define human thoughts.

3

Sensation

The Mind Is Not All in the Brain

The process of transforming raw sensation into clear and distinct perceptions is performed by a complex hierarchy of simultaneously operating neural nets that stretch from the highest levels of the brain down to the sensory organs themselves.

Many of these nets are in place at birth, but most must be programmed by experience—they must learn to perceive. The specialized neural nets that perceive the environment often preprocess that raw sensation into discernible objects before even notifying the conscious mind.

The mind is familiar with the objects of vision, hearing, touch, taste, and smell because they are prepackaged as such by an ascending hierarchy of neural nets in the brain, beginning with the sensory organs themselves.

Synthetic sensory organs, equipped to be similarly cognizant of objects, are among the essential cognizer subsystems. In the brain, these mechanisms have been layered upon one another by millennia of evolution. In cognizers, they must be painstakingly built up.

When Aristotle pronounced that the brain's probable function was to cool the blood, he was being consistent with the ideas that will, judgment, and human reason were ethereal entities not to be identified with the body. For nearly 2000 years, the true function of the brain remained obscure. Even the seventeenth century's grand doubter, René Descartes, thought that consciousness was so fine a substance that it would fit inside the pituitary gland. Descartes' big advancement of human understanding was to pronounce that the rest of the brain was a repository of memories, each one of which left a *trace*.

Today many researchers still believe in the memory trace. Even though the pituitary gland was found to be the source of a growth hormone, the concept of the *self* as being *in the head* has remained. To this day, many people continue to identify the brain with the self. The mind has come to be thought of not only as material, but also as the brain itself.

This kind of thinking was encouraged by work being done on mapping out brain functions. In 1870, two German physicians, Gustav Fritsch and Edward Hitzig, had an opportunity to experiment on patients whose brains were exposed by gunshot wounds. By stimulating the exposed brains of their patients, these Germans successfully isolated the area of the brain accountable to the eyes. They found that even minute electric shocks could cause the patients' eyes to move.

The pair later reconfirmed and expanded on their findings at home, allegedly by cutting holes through the skulls of dogs while they lay anesthetized on Mrs. Hitzig's dressing table. These crude experiments demonstrated that for both man and animal, well-defined areas of the brain were in charge of muscular movement.

Those findings were later confirmed in England by scientist David Ferrier, who showed that in monkeys the wrinkled outer surface of the brain was mainly devoted to the control of the various muscles.

Searching for the "I"

By the early twentieth century, the belief reined that the brain itself was the seat of consciousness. Descartes' memory traces had been renamed *engrams* by the French scientist, Richard Sermon, and the search was on for finding the stuff of thought inside the head.

University of Michigan researcher James Olds found an area in the brain of rats that acted as a pleasure center. When he wired up this area so that a rat could stimulate it by stepping on a button, he found that rats would respond as many as 5000 times per hour, neglecting all else, even food.

Another researcher made a similarly startling discovery about human brains. Canadian brain surgeon Wilder Penfield discovered that electrodes touched to various areas of the brain of a conscious patient stimulated memories. People remembered situations, and heard and saw things that weren't there but had happened in the past. Because he could initiate the same memories over and over merely by restimulating the precise brain area, Penfield thought he had found the engram.

Other researchers began duplicating Penfield's work in animals with astounding success. A Spaniard, Josê Delgado, wired up a bull with a radio-controlled electrode buried in its pleasure center. When the bull charged Delgado, he fearlessly stood his ground until just before the bull gored him, then used his radio-controlled simulator to cause the bull to lose interest.

It appeared that soon the brain's memory and perceptual apparatus would be deciphered. And though a great deal has been learned about the various structures of the brain and the functions they perform, very little is understood about how the brain actually does what it does.

Neurons Thinking for Themselves

In 1959, however, researchers at the Massachusetts Institute of Technology (MIT) dashed the hopes for an easy solution by showing that the higher levels of the brain were only a part of the story of cognition. At first, the proposed theory sounded like a resurrection of Descartes' theory of the pituitary gland. The difference was that this assertion could be backed up by laboratory evidence. Neural networks outside the brain—in the organs and through several levels of processing—appeared to do their own thinking.

Warren McCulloch, Walter Pitts, J. Y. Lettvin and H. R. Maturana at MIT demonstrated that a frog's eye actually packaged perceptions into objects before sending notification up to the conscious levels of the brain. Notably, the eye itself appeared to be able to recognize flying bugs, for instance, and send the message *There's a bug!* up to its brain. Of course, without the brain not much good could come of such an alert; nevertheless the actual detection is done in the eye.

Before McCulloch and Pitts, researchers viewed the eye as a television camera which sends raw sensory data up to the brain for high-level pattern-matching operations. But the MIT experiments showed that the neurons in the body are not so very different from those of the brain. In frogs, bug perception is probably triggered by detectors in the eye. In cats, the recognition of sharp edges also appears to be performed in the eye. Researchers have subsequently identified over 50 different types of receptor cells in the human eye.

Anatomy of a Sense Organ

The first clue came for the MIT researchers when they noticed that not all the neural sensory receptors in the eye reacted the same way to the same stimulus. They were able to isolate several types of neural formations, each specialized to fulfill a certain function in the frog. One formation appeared to recognize flying insects, no matter what else was in its visual field.

When a flying insect entered the scene, these formations began sending a short message up to the brain—too short, the MIT group reasoned, to be an image.

Try as they might, they could not fool the frog's eye either. It would not react to pictures of insects, though it was indiscriminate as to whether the moving speck was dead or alive. Another formation in the frog's eye was found to detect sharp edges whether they were moving or stationary. Yet another would react only to moving edges.

These and later experiments by D. H. Hubel and T. N. Wiesel at the Harvard Medical School confirmed that eyes do not just convey a visual field to the brain, as a television camera feeds a computer, but that the eye itself recognized objects.

In order to determine whether or not brain neurons acted like eye neurons, the Harvard researchers attached electrodes to individual neurons in the brains of cats. They found that, in the brain, individual receiving neurons appeared to specialize in detecting certain object types. Many of these types, such as moving edges, were found to function similarly to their analogs in the eye.

Further investigations showed that individual neurons, no matter where they were located, appeared to think for themselves, at least to some limited degree. A California Institute of Technology researcher, Cornelius Wiersma, separately confirmed that notion by showing that an individual crayfish neuron could detect light coming from above. That neuron was even smart enough to be able to detect light whether the crayfish was right side up or upside down. Thus, these individual neurons were cognizant of the pull of gravity! These and other more recent studies have led scientists to the belief that individual neurons are at least as smart as the kind of microprocessor chip that runs the garden-variety automated teller machine (ATM).

Do Brains Correspond to Minds?

Even though individual neurons possess the ability to perform complex operations in and of themselves, the emergence of mind from brain states is the result of a complex systematic cooperation among neurons. In the long and convoluted pathways from raw sensation to clear and distinct perceptions, several levels of organization exist, each one of which adds its own a priori categorization to raw experience.

The categories of experience, partly learned and partly encoded in the architecture of the nervous system, can be mapped out in neural anatomy. But the precise functioning of these neural structures is only now being supported by theoretical underpinnings robust enough in mathematics to explain them.

The brain is not the sole repository of the stuff of consciousness. The subject matter of consciousness—the objects of sensation and emotion—are the products of an almost haphazard array of neural networks stretching from the sense organs up to the neurons of the brain. The various elements of this hierarchy appear to have evolved over millions of years, and the entire network of neurons, including those in specific organs of the body, sifts the information that eventually enters the conscious levels of the mind.

Neurons in the sense organs pass raw sensation through several levels of analysis to glean a whole variety of perceptions from a single stimuli. These successive levels conclude by dumping a conglomeration of perceptions into short-term memory. Those perceptions include both a summary of the current objects being perceived and a set of memories and emotions stimulated by association. This simultaneous stimulation can range from simple feature extraction ("that is a line") to complex pattern recognition ("Great, there's Lisa; I was looking for her.")

From birth to death, a human's neural networks grapple with a changing base of sense experience from which to congeal images into objects and form emotional opinions. The various mechanisms in the brain appear to have evolved at different times, giving a remarkable variety to the perceptual modes. Some, like breathing, are built-in to the most primitive part of the brain stem. Others, like the "fight or flight" reaction, also appear to be built-in, but are the result of an assembly of structures in the brain. Still others, such as aesthetic appreciation, are thought to be a part of the newest brain structures, principally the outer cerebral cortex.

All these structures are active simultaneously, the old and the new existing side by side. Primitive impulses, emotional considerations, and high-level reasoning all compete for dominance in modern man. The different time scales, from immediate reflex reactions to emotional trauma to reasoned conclusions, each have their place since the higher level structures were slowly layered on top of the old.

Perception Arises from Sensation

When perceiving the environment, the conscious levels of the mind get but an executive summary of what senses take in and associate with prior experience. The senses are connected to an ascending hierarchy of neural networks that preprocesses the visual, auditory, and tactile information before passing it on to the conscious levels of the mind. Hundreds of varieties of specialized neurons perform the same sort of operations for each of the senses, as well as satisfy the body's own internal needs.

The flow of information within the hierarchy of neural networks is from sense organs into the midbrain. The spinal cord collects information from the body and sends it up to the brain stem. Each vertebrae admits between its segments the nerve fibers from local sense organs, a fact which explains the pinched nerve that sometimes afflicts those with back pain.

At the brain stem, various structures, including the surrounding cerebellum, control bodily functions—from heart rate to posture. These are the oldest structures in the brain. What evolved later, on top of them, are most of the controlling structures that coordinate current perceptions, short-term memory, and emotional reactions.

The last part of the brain to evolve, the cerebrum, is assumed to be the site of intelligence. The cerebrum, divided into two parts joined by the corpus callosum, consists of an underlying mass of *white matter* that is intricately connected to the *gray matter,* or cerebral cortex. The cortex is thought to contain the codes that allow perceptions to be stored in long-term memory. The cerebral cortex also is assumed to be the key to the mind's ability to associate previously gathered knowledge with new experiences—learning.

Long years of experimenting with humans and monkeys has revealed a detailed map of the various parts and apparent functions of the cerebral cortex. Each portion of the cortex appears to be dedicated to a particular manner of dealing with the world. Visual sensation originates in the cortex at the back of the head and feeds forward toward the temporal area and the parietal lobe, presumably assembling a world view.

Two bands across the top of the head appear to receive stimulation from the body's surface sensors for pressure, heat, pain, and other tactile sensations, with one small fold beneath the temporal lobe handling hearing. The frontal lobe appears to function with long range planning operations and other high-level cognition. Patients who have received lobotomies—removal or laceration of frontal lobes—experience the elimination of both the ability and drive to achieve complex future goals.

The cerebral cortex itself is just one-eighth of an inch thick. Within that thickness are several layers, penetrated from top to bottom by thin slabs of neurons. The outside layers appear to feed downward along these slabs toward more abstract forms of pattern recognition. For instance, a single slab might relate to a certain part of the visual field, with deeper layers extracting features and object information. Dendrites from one slab will occasionally stray into adjacent slabs, but for the most part, the neurons of the cortex work in flat, autonomous sheets or slabs.

The cortex, the so-called gray matter, is thoroughly connected to the rest of the deep brain structures from beneath by the fibrous white matter. The white matter serves as the information highway between the cortex and older structures of the brain that regulate bodily activities, gather sensory information, and evoke emotional responses. The white matter can also handle

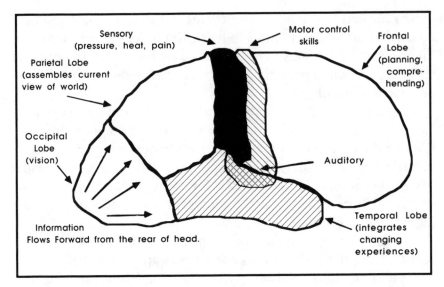

Sensation to Perception. Sensation probes the cortex retrieving knowledge from past experience to form perceptions. Visual information sweeps from rear forward with the most complex functions, such as planning, performed in the frontal lobes of the cortex.

the complex chain of activities that starts with a conscious volition to perform some action and results in mobilizing resources to do it.

Many of the structures in the middle of the brain also mediate cognition. The thalamus, for instance, appears to be the brain's central controlling mechanism. It receives raw sensation from the senses as well as from memories of past experiences. As the center of consciousness, the thalamus appears to relate new experiences to the appropriate portions of the cerebral cortex for association with past experiences.

The thalamus is surrounded by the limbic system that directly connects to the cerebral cortex via a mass of white matter. This comprehensive interconnection scheme links the central controlling mechanisms to the accumulated knowledge residing in the cerebral cortex. The various parts of the limbic system form an integrated controlling mechanism that responds to the outside world in whatever manner is appropriate. The hippocampus,

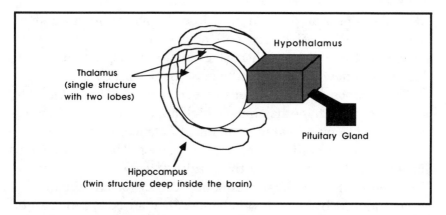

Thalamus. The thalamus is one of the older parts of the mid brain and acts as a central controller. Many researchers also believe that the thalamus is likely the controller of iconic memory (only a 1/10th of a second long) and short-term memory (up to 15 seconds long).

which spirals around the thalamus and terminates in the hypothalamus, appears to be instrumental in transforming short-term memories into long-term memories.

The shortest form of memory, called *iconic,* is nearly photographic in quality, but unless reinforced, it lasts for just a fraction of a second. For instance, the iconic memory can store a telephone number long enough for you to get it written down one digit at a time, but in order to keep the number in mind long enough to dial the phone, short-term memory must kick in.

Short-term memories are not as clear and distinct as iconic memories, but they last several seconds (about 15) without reinforcement. By repeating the number to oneself, these short-term memories can be constantly reinforced and thus remembered as long as repetition is continued.

Whenever the associations between current experience and the past are strong enough to reinforce short-term memories on their own, these short-term memories are incorporated into long-term memory. Memory training courses teach their pupils to associate consciously an item to be remembered with an existing memory, thus fixing it in long-term memory. This operation is performed, apparently, by the hippocampus since patients with the hippocampus removed lose the ability to store short-term memories. They are still able to reason about current events and associate with past events, but they are unable to learn from new experiences because they can not store them.

The hippocampus also feeds directly into the emotional control center, the hypothalamus, which appears to control eating, drinking, sleeping, waking, chemical balances, heart rate, hormones, sex, and other emotional responses. The hypothalamus in turn feeds directly into the pituitary gland which seems to function as the chemical production center for emotional reactions induced by the hypothalamus. In many ways, these hormones and other chemicals create the *texture* of thought.

Japan's Neuroscientist

As director of Japan's only neurological research center, Hideo Sakata feels qualified to speculate on the function of the hippocampus. Sakata began his work with the study of spatial perception in apes; after years of study, one of his most profound conclusions is that the hippocampus is the key to memory in the brain and that it controls the association cortex.

The hippocampus, according to Sakata, is a structure for rehearsal in memory. It gathers the various association information stimulated by sensation and circulates it in order to reinforce and store it in the association cortex. The hippocampus gathers this information from various areas, each of which stores a specific kind of information, and integrates this information—affixing relationships, performing data compression and time sequencing—for proper identification of sensory inputs.

At the time of birth, the association cortex is not yet developed. People are born with only a very small number of areas already developed, such as visual areas. Most of the structures inside, like the hypothalamus, are merely relay stations. But when fully developed, very complicated patterns can be recognized by single or very small groups of neurons, a fact which suggests to Sakata that very small regions of the brain are the sights of memory.

The Seat of Consciousness

As an age-old candidate for the *seat of consciousness,* the thalamus and its associated limbic system are surrounded by the mass of fibrous white matter that connects them to the higher centers in the cerebral cortex. The very oldest brain structures

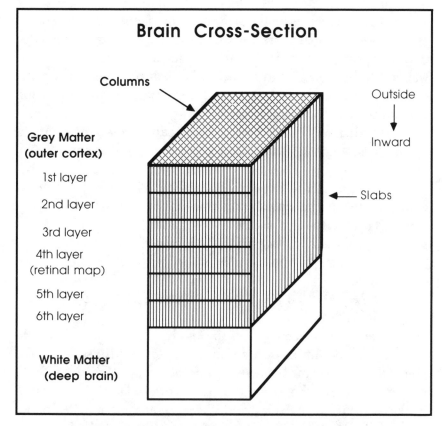

Columns from Slabs. The one-eighth inch thick outer cortex is based on columns of neurons that ascend in layers of increasingly refined cognition. For vision, many orientations of an object (upside down, turned on its side, etc.) can be recognized by vertical columns.

below the thalamus still regulate the bodily functions, but their highest activities now consist of coordinating learned motor functions, such as riding a bicycle or tying a shoe.

It now appears that the outer cortex of the brain performs much of the pattern recognition for the conscious mind. The structures that physiologists have uncovered which support this argument are based on the slabs and their constituent columns of cells. These columns penetrate the cortex from outside, passing through several layers of tissue. Of the various levels of the cortex, six distinct layers have been identified so far. The outer layer appears to deal with very primordial forms of sensation while higher level associations occur at deeper layers. For instance, some researchers now believe that a map of the sense organs is mirrored on level four. The levels below level four are thought to be feature extractors and object recognition regions. Columns of cells are thought to differentiate between possible orientations of the same feature.

No one has yet combined the intricate known mapping of brain physiology with a strong theoretical underpinning. The precise division of labor between sense organs and the various levels of the brain is not yet established. Physiologists tend to concentrate on the processing that happens inside the brain, whereas theorists concentrate on findings that indicate the sense organs themselves perform cognitive functions.

Japanese Attack Column Mystery

One Japanese researcher who thinks that he has elucidated the function of column structures in the brain is NEC's Kenji Okajima. Okajima has built a self-organizing model of visual pattern recognition that is based on the early work of D. H. Hubel and T. N. Wiesel. But, while Hubel and Wiesel thought that cells formed columns for detecting line segments, Okajima now believes that the whole object is represented by a complex cloud of cells.

If Okajima is correct, he has explained why neural networks can recognize objects regardless of the angle at which they are perceived. The whole three-dimensional object, from every angle, is encoded in a single two-dimensional and in some cases one-dimensional site in the brain. The same set of cells recognize the object no matter the angle from which it is perceived.

Okajima claims that columns are stable with regard to shifts in position without any loss in resolution, because the components of the pattern are preserved throughout the process.

Building Cognizant Sensory Apparatus

Among those who concentrate on the intelligence inherent in the sense organs themselves, a group of technologists have emerged who could revolutionize synthetic sensors for cognizers, vision and speech recognition systems, in particular.

By separating the resolution of objects from reasoning about them, the new theories challenge traditional artificial-intelligence (AI) recognition systems. Instead of attempting to emulate high-level geometric or linguistic concepts with conventional AI rules, the new approach uses systems of differential equations that describe the low-level electrical behavior of the nerve networks themselves. The high-level conceptual modeling now appears to be unnecessary, since these qualities tend to emerge automatically once a massive enough number of low-level connections are made properly.

These techniques have arisen from studies of the dynamics of biological competitive growth among neural cells. Biological systems, it appears, break a continuous perceptual field into meaningful units and organize them into pictures or sounds or tastes or smells or textures, according the structure of the sensory receptor and its corresponding brain centers.

A large number of neurons operate autonomously on the incoming sensory data, each competing with neighbors for dominance at their respective locations throughout the hierarchy of brain levels. For example, cells have a slightly different sensitivity to the orientation of light reflected off a line or edge at any given angle. Some are strongly excited from a specific orientation, while nearby ones will respond with markedly less activity.

These competing cells are linked to one another in a complex hierarchy of connections. At each level, the cells that are responding most vigorously to a given stimuli will try to take over that level of the hierarchy. The group that dominates gets to send a message to the next level. The greatest competition for dominance occurs at the lower levels of the hierarchy. As the stimulus works its way up to higher levels, cooperation begins, and the dominating signals are organized into coherent images.

From birth to death, eyes and their corresponding brain centers learn about their environment and adapt to its changing circumstances. It is this competition for dominance by autonomous agents connected in a complex hierarchy that allows man to learn and adapt. Experience molds our neural nets to immediate needs.

Perceptron Perfected

One Japanese researcher has been quietly perfecting the first popular neural network called the *perceptron*. Kunihiko Fukushima at NHK Laboratories developed his first successor to the perceptron, the *cognitron*, nearly 10 years ago. The cognitron was designed to recognize symbols from any alphabet after being trained merely by having the symbols presented to it.

But the cognitron was found to have a deficiency. It could not recognize patterns that were shifted in position or distorted. Consequently, Fukushima sought a way to recognize things distorted in shape and shifted in position. Thus, the *neocognitron* was born.

The neocognitron is a multistage pattern-recognizer/feature-extractor that simulates the way visual information feeds forward in cortex. It uses successive stages of cells that are very similar to Rosenblatt's original layers. The many stages allow the neocognitron to recognize patterns regardless of position or distortion. As sensation goes through successive stages, the position of the symbols in the visual field becomes less and less important. On the highest level, patterns are unique and distinct, but as the successive stages are activated, a given symbol tends to stimulate the same cells regardless of how it is shifted or distorted. Eventually a stage is reached where only a single cell reacts for each training pattern.

Carver Mead's Eyeball

By looking at the first layer of neurons behind the eye's photodetectors, CalTech researcher Carver Mead realized that their function was to provide inhibitory feedback to enhance motion detection. The eye registers light intensity changes as the movement is detected, not later when comparing successive images.

According to Mead, nature realized that it was economical to do motion processing before passing information on to the brain. It's just too costly to attempt to reconstruct movement after the data is collected. When the object is moving, it is constantly providing clues to direction, speed and so forth. Once the image is frozen and sent "upstairs" for processing, the motion is gone. It would take a supercomputer to reconstruct motion information from a series of images.

In the eye, the first layer of pure photoreceptors registers temporal rate-of-change information which is then passed to further layers of neurons for feature extraction before the impulses are channeled to the higher cognitive centers in the brain. This elegant system reveals a chain of processing that continuously modifies the information it tracks in accordance with changes in the nature of the environment. There isn't time to process individual snapshots of the environment in order to reconstruct the motion information among them. Instead, the eye capitalizes on the nature of real-world input which continually provides this information. It is not necessary or even desirable to store away raw image information when it is always available.

According to Mead, this kind of processing on the fly represents the overwhelming bulk of neural activity in the brain. The

Carver Mead. Already a star in microchips—co-inventor of the "silicon compiler" (software that automatically designs microchips)—Carver Mead has made neural circuitry his life's work at Synaptics Inc., along with co-founding microprocessor innovator Federico Faggin.

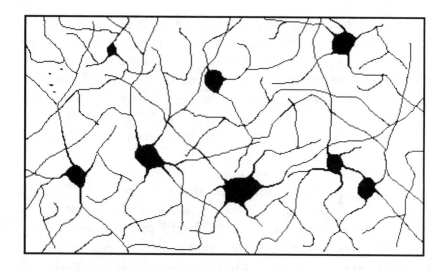

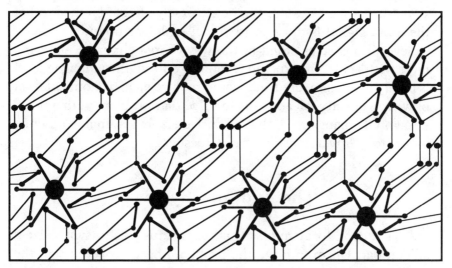

Mead's Eyeball. Carver Mead's microchip version of the peripheral-vision neural network in the eyeball (bottom) has a striking resemblance to the eye's actual neural network (top). At Synaptics Inc., Mead hopes to bring such microchips to the marketplace.

eye and the other sense organs appear to do more than record raw sensation for the brain to process. Since the raw information is right there for the having, it does not need to be recorded. What the sense organs do need to do is sift through that vast influx of raw information to extract the features that are important, such as "bug alert, food is nearby!" Mead refers to this phenomenon as the *neural iceberg beneath the cognitive tip of conscious thought.*

Having built his artificial retina, Mead moved on to model the next layer behind the retina—the amicrine layer. The function of this layer, according to Mead, is to add a spatial analysis to the time dimension analysis of the first layer. This second processing step enhances the perception of motion by allowing the system to scale its response to the average level of input. Any signal-processing system can be adversely affected if the level of the input signal is close to its upper or lower bounds.

Several obstacles stand in the way of modeling the amicrine layer with analog microchip technology. First, the amicrine level is highly interconnected and would require an astronomical level of wiring density. Mead plans to solve that problem with a novel hexagonal wiring layout that he derived from seminal work done by Boston University's Stephen Grossberg.

The Auditory System

Mead's second foray into sensory apparatus was to synthesize a silicon ear. On examining the problem, he discovered that the auditory system evolved before there were speaking animals. Thus, the auditory system could not have been designed to understand speech, but rather was engineered to localize and identify sounds. Mead also found that auditory research revealed several clues as to how the auditory system localizes sounds.

The mechanisms appeared to be well understood. Sounds are localized separately in the horizontal and vertical planes, with localization in the horizontal plane best understood. In the horizontal plane, localization is done with stereo cues from transients that come to one ear before the other. This phenomenon is known as the *interaural time-delay cue*. The horizontal distance between the two ears yields a time delay of about 700 microseconds.

Another less well-known but equally important cue for horizontal localization is that the ear aimed toward a sound gets more high frequencies than the one facing away from the sound. This cue is called the *head-shadow* and is a very powerful mechanism, often as strong as the interaural time-delay cue. The interaural time-delay cue and the head-shadow cue together yield localization in the horizontal plane.

Vertical localization of sound is more difficult but can be accomplished because there are two paths into the ear canal, one that goes directly to the ear drum and one that deflects off the sides of the canal as it enters. The delay because of the deflected path depends upon the vertical angle from which the sound comes. The time delay cue for vertical perception is only about 70 microseconds, making it weaker, but still clearly perceptible.

Modeling the Ear

In order to duplicate this localization machinery in silicon, Mead has built several chips based on a detailed analysis of the ear's structural dynamics. The translation between the sound waves that come into the head and the electrical impulses that feed the brain occurs in the *cochlea*, a snail-shaped structure which is filled with fluid. The cochlea is divided into three chambers by membranes, the most important of which is called the *basilar membrane*. The fluid is incompressible so that pressure on one membrane displaces both the fluid and the other membrane.

The basilar membrane divides the cochlea along most of its length, leaving an opening at the end. The stiffness of the membrane varies along its length, decreasing by about two orders of magnitude over 3 or 4 cm.

When the membrane vibrates, a pressure difference develops between the fluid above it and the fluid below, a difference that starts a wave traveling down its length. The velocity of the wave is proportional to the stiffness of the membrane. The wave travels very rapidly at the beginning and then slows down as the stiffness decreases.

As the wave slows down, the energy per unit time remains constant, but the energy density per unit distance gets larger. To compensate, the amplitude of the wave grows as the wavelength gets shorter. In other words, the waves pile up as the waveform gets very tall and narrow and second order properties of the membrane damp it out. That loss in the membrane cuts off the high frequencies very rapidly.

By studying the membrane itself, Mead found that the stiffness decreases exponentially with distance, accounting for the subjective perception of sound as logarithmic. That is, the frequency scale is exponential. For instance, if the frequency of a wave is a multiple of the original, then exactly the same wave is formed, it is just shifted over to the right or left on the logarithmic scale. Mead contends that this step is the first in understanding the octave relationship.

According to Mead's analysis, hearing has built into it an invariance against harmonics because of the exponential characteristics of the cochlea. If the frequency of a sound wave is doubled, then the spatial pattern on the membrane for that wave is the same as for the original, just shifted over. If it is doubled again, then the new membrane pattern is also identical, just moved over again by the same amount. Thus, the octave relationship is built into the aural representation at the very lowest level of mechanical transduction in the hearing system.

Basilar Membrane Details

After the sound pressure from the outside world is transformed into a traveling wave along the basilar membrane, four rows of hair cells or cilia above the fluid-filled cochlea sense the rate at which the membrane vibrates. The inner row of these hairs move as little as an angstrom to change the firing rate of the neural cells to which they are attached. These neural cells then feed ganglia that attach to the auditory nerve which goes up to the brain. If these hairs are ever dislodged by loud noises, such as gunshots or shrill guitar solos, they do not grow back.

The outer three rows of these hair cells are fastened in a stationary position above the membrane to exert a force on it like a muscle. As the membrane rocks back and forth, the mechanical motion stimulates those cilia to apply a force back onto the membrane so as to lower the mechanical damping of the system. The result is a negative mechanical resistance, or positive feedback. There are enough hair cells to cause the mechanism to become so active that it produces a spontaneous mechanical oscillation—ringing in the ear such as when one stretches in the morning.

This active feedback demonstrates that the ear is set up to hear transients. The cochlea creates a traveling wave structure that preserves the transient nature of sound. The mechanical feedback is controlled by efferent fibers coming down from the brain to the cochlea. The efferent fibers are a very complex and sophisticated feedback system that can turn down the mechanical gain of the outer hair cells. When there is lots of sound information coming in, the automatic gain signals are computed up in the olivary complex, and feedback signals, which are very slow compared to the auditory signal, are sent to turn down the gain.

Chips Like the Ear

The first microchip to be built was a traveling wave structure that is a silicon analog of the cochlea. A transmission line was made out of 480 amplifiers wired together serially. Each delay element had to charge two capacitors. By decreasing the damping of the traveling wave structure, one amplifier going backwards, within each delay element, provided the positive feedback corresponding to the action of an outer hair cell. A linear voltage gradient on the exponential gain control terminals of each amplifier was the silicon trick that modeled perfectly the exponential decrease in stiffness along the basilar membrane. Mead has also built a silicon version of a hair cell.

Mead contends that there are a lot of stages between the cochlea and high-level operations like speech recognition, and he predicts that it will take 10 years to map out all the information-processing steps between the senses and the outer cortex.

4

The Necessary Insight

Fathering the Cognizer Revolution

While several promising lines of research have come out of attempts to understand the brain, it took the combined insight of scientists doing basic research in mathematics, biology, physics, and computer science to craft the cognizer.

Research scientists have managed to build a bridge between neural biology and electronic-circuit theory, bringing both fields into focus with the lens of mathematical physics.

The insight necessary to begin cracking the brain's mysteries has not come from physicians and psychologists but from philosophers, mathematicians, and physicists who were speculating on the nature and function of cognition long before the necessary tools were available to solve the puzzle. Medical men have supplied the many clues, but only a joint effort among scientific disciplines could penetrate the complexity of the problem.

Computer scientists are the most recent members of these multidisciplinary research teams. Like other technological artifacts of the scientific revolution, the computer was conceived as an aid to the advancement of science and society. But the act of refining computer design has brought about insights that were unimaginable when the computer was invented.

There are many examples of this kind of activity in other fields. For instance thermodynamics (the study of heat transfer) has gone far beyond its original intention—the design of steam engines. It has been refined and generalized over the past 150 years until it is now applied to virtually any physical system. The computer—along with other electronic devices like radio, television, and the telephone—has spawned a new theory of information. Unremarkably, information theory bears a strong resemblance to thermodynamic theory—both describe how a single underlying quantity is transformed by machines.

In thermodynamics, this quantity is energy. In the operation of a railroad train, for instance, energy is released when coal burns and is transferred to the water in a engine's boiler, turning the water into steam. The steam is then channeled to the pistons which drive the wheels of the train. A steam engine is thus able to extract the potential energy in an inert substance and transform it into the dynamics of a railroad train.

The concept of information received the same treatment at Bell Laboratories in the 1940s when two scientists, Claude Shannon and Warren Weaver, published a paper showing that information could be quantified and its various forms described by mathematical laws. Shannon and Weaver's new *information theory* created a sensation. One reason it did was that, according to the theory, information closely resembles energy, a resemblance that was the subject of many philosophical treatises and popular articles.

Put simply, the thesis went like this: Just as coal is turned into mechanical work in a steam engine, modern electronic devices transform information from one form to another. For example, compact disks (CDs) can be thought of as the information analogs of coal. The minute variations on these disks are transformed into an electrical signal that is fed to high-fidelity speakers so that our auditory system can convert the signals into electric currents that perform work in the brain. Just as one can transform the potential energy in coal into useful work. Shannon and Weaver quantified information instead of horsepower merely by numbering the symbols representing it and connecting them with equations.

Information theory has typically been physical in its orientation. Although one might react to it in a variety of subjective ways, information was viewed as a purely objective quantity. The qualitative differences in reading a play, viewing a television drama, or listening to a symphony have little to do with the invariant quantities an information theorist would assign to all of these forms of information. From the physicist's point of view, the power of the theory comes from the ability to ignore the infinite variety of information content. Shakespeare's *Hamlet* or Lewis Carroll's *Jabberwocky* would be described by the same equations.

However, while information theory might be viewed as a cornerstone of the information revolution, it is not the entire structure. There are basic inadequacies in treating information as if its content were irrelevant. Scientists and technologists have had to add their own extensions to the theory as they have forged new information tools that more accurately describe reality. A purely syntactic definition of information—one that ignores meaning (semantics)—cannot fully describe electronic information processing because the information processed is inextricably intertwined with meaning. The content of an information channel *does* have an impact on both the quantity and quality of real information it transmits.

This fact was first pointed out in the 1960s by Pietre Jacobus van Heerden, a physicist at Polaroid Laboratories. Van Heerden concocted a simple paradox for the objective measure of information proposed by Shannon and Weaver. He defined the information content of a line of text simply as the number of characters the line contains, a definition analogous to that of Shannon and Weaver. Using this measurement method, the information content of a word with eight characters is simply eight.

Now, consider the sequence of characters 3.1415926 . . . Van Heerdon's method of information measurement would assign the value eight as a measure of this line's information content. But if this sequence were received by someone educated in elementary mathematics, he might notice that these particular digits are the first eight digits of the constant π. This educated observer could be sent the equivalent message π, with an information content of one, from which he could construct the indefinitely long sequence of information content ∞. To receive the same amount of information, an uneducated observer would need the whole string of characters.

This example revealed the complexity that lay beneath a simple attempt to apply physical analyses to information technology. Computers compound the problem since they not only transmit and store data, but also have the ability to execute programs. Yet both data and programs are treated identically by information theory.

The above example shows how a compact program (π) can substitute for a long, voluminous string of bare information. This raises the interesting question of how one can recognize the difference between a sequence of truly random characters and a pseudo-random sequence with some underlying pattern. The answer van Heerden gave was simple: One cannot. Information measures are dependent on who or what is receiving the information.

Insights drawn from biology may eventually resolve this complex dilemma. Physicists have been perplexed and enthralled by biological systems for centuries. But the two sciences have been very different in method and philosophical orientation. In many ways, biological systems represent an ultimate challenge both to information theory and physics. They are constructed of the same matter as air, rocks, and water, yet they seem infinitely more complex and varied. Within these complex processes lies the ultimate mystery: *consciousness*. Because biology ultimately is a physical process, the physicist faces the task of explaining our inner thoughts in terms of the equations of physics.

Classical physicists like Hermann von Helmholtz, Ernst Mach, and James Maxwell were preoccupied with biological systems. Modern physicists like Niels Bohr, John von Neumann, and Norbert Weiner also made bold attempts to understand biology as a physical phenomenon. None have succeeded, although they could not be accused of failure either. The problem is simply too big to discount any small achievements made toward solving it.

Von Neumann's Secret Obsession

John von Neumann, the father of the modern digital computer, made significant contributions to mathematics and quantum theory as well as to computer science from 1930, when he came to the United States from Hungary, until his death in 1957. The final obsession of his life, however, was biological in nature —reproduction. Biological systems are built from systematic organizations of self-replicating cells. Could machines—automata—ever reach the stage of self replication?

Von Neumann's early career focused on elucidating computer design with a comprehensive theory of computation. Since he had modeled that computer theory on his notion of how biological systems work, it was inevitable that he eventually attempt to simulate the ability of biological systems to reproduce. The reproduction mechanism is fundamental, not only to our adaptability to changing environments as a species, but also to our growth as individuals. All creatures begin as a single cell which continuously divides, creating innumerable replicas of itself. All the diverse organs in our bodies, including the billions of neurons, are simply specialized versions of this one cell. Could automata simulate such a mechanism?

Von Neumann created several models that showed how automatic machines, similar to the formal computers created by Alan Turing, could simulate the act of self-replication. Turing machines read an input tape that contained a finite set of symbols and used rules to transform the information read into symbols written on an output tape. Turing had already shown this simple formal machine to be equivalent to, albeit much slower than any conceivable computer, digital or analog. Von

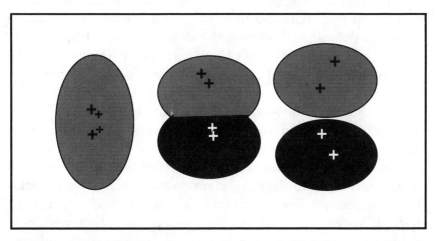

Dividing Cells. Cell-replication—the ability to make nearly identical copies of oneself—distinguishes living organisms from inanimate objects. Living cells usually perform this miracle by doubling and then splitting their genetic materials into identical, yet autonomous, cells.

Neumann showed how a certain set of these rules—a program—could be used to instruct a Turing machine to create exact duplicates of itself.

In essence, von Neumann was attempting to apply the thesis proposed by Alonzo Church a decade earlier that any effective process in the physical world could be simulated with a suitable Turing machine. Von Neumann argued that there must be a universal automata constructor—a physical system that could build copies of itself—because he could show a formal simulation of one using Turing machines. Thus von Neumann's *self-replicating automata*, as he called them, involved the familiar reductionist equivocation between simulations and models. He assumed the reductionist position that a physical constructor could *model* biological self-replication because a *simulation* of a constructor could be made with Turing machines.

This reductionist equivalence between the notion of automatic control and biological reproduction was reinforced soon after von Neumann's death. In the early 1960s, biologists discovered the DNA molecule that stores the information cells use to reproduce themselves.

The similarity was uncanny. Further work by reductionist scientists showed that the mechanisms of DNA reproduction matched the mechanism von Neumann proposed in his self-replicating rules for Turing's formal computer. The cell read the DNA molecule just as if it were a Turing machine's input tape. DNA even had a finite set of symbols—pairs of peptide molecules—similar to the alphabet of a Turing machine. These symbols were interpreted by chemical processes in the cell in order to manufacture amino acids, proteins and the other building blocks used in self-replication. The resemblance to von Neumann's self-reproducing automata was so uncanny that it quickly led biologists to view everything in a human body, except the nervous system, as an assemblage of organic Turing machines.

The nervous system, though, was a second, entirely different network that is superimposed on the basic assemblage of biological cells. Researchers even found two kinds of DNA molecules, one for nerve cells—neurons—and one for the other cells. The time scale for the operation of the two systems was radically different as well. Evolution requires millions of years to adapt and change the makeup of DNA, but complex nervous systems could adapt and learn new ways of coping with the environment almost immediately. Reductionist scientists at first hoped that, by building simulations of the two types of mechanisms and replicating them astronomically, artificial neural networks might produce synthetic intelligence. But the purely syntactic operations of computer simulations ignored the semantic content of information as surely as Shannon and Weaver did.

The nervous system does not merely operate according to a program, even if DNA does. The semantic content of learned descriptions of experience endows the objects of perception with a meaning that cannot be encoded into a computer program. But cognizers, it would later be discovered, could truly model the nervous system by gleaning meaning from the world in the same manner that natural neural networks do—that is, by learning.

Hopfield's Insight

> . . . the real mysteries of biology lie in the way in which . . .
> dynamical laws of physics and the substrate of electrons, photons,
> and nuclei on which they operate, produce the complex set of
> counter-intuitive phenomena labeled with the term biology.
> **John Hopfield** (1986)

Modern breakthroughs in the understanding of the physical mechanisms of life have begun with information theory. Informational models provide some important clues as to how biological systems organize and operate in a highly unpredictable and random environment, but the deficiencies of these models also quickly became apparent.

In the early 1980s, John Hopfield, a physicist at California Institute of Technology, began to study the similarities and differences between biological processes and electronic computation. Rather than describe his findings as noncomputational,

John Hopfield. More than anyone else California Institute of Technology physicist John Hopfield has revitalized neural network research. Hopfield started analyzing the similarities and differences between biological and electronic computation in the early 1980s.

however, Hopfield created a hierarchy of increasing computational complexity, concluding that the brain is a biocomputer that performs *collective computation.*

Despite the way it sounds, this classification scheme is not reductionist. Hopfield clearly understands the difference between simulations and models but simply chooses to redefine *computation* to apply to both. His most significant work has been to model—*not* simulate—real neural networks with electronic materials. Hopfield has also carefully catalogued the differences between what he calls biological computation and the formal computation of computer programs. For instance, computers cannot generally tolerate error. While computer engineers have devised various fault-tolerant mechanisms to make computers more reliable, no computer can handle the error rates of a real neural network. The brain, on the other hand, can tolerate the death of millions of neurons without the slightest disturbance, can recover from massive damage and even reconstruct information that was lost in the catastrophe.

Hopfield pointed out that any system which computes according to a program must have some way of dealing with errors. Since random effects are always going to interfere with the path to the correct solution, computation must always involve mechanisms that restore the course of a physical system to its correct path. Computer engineers have spent entire careers developing techniques to restore digital computers to their correct computational course, techniques such as continually refreshing the logical values in a dynamic memory to prevent their deterioration over time.

Hopfield has devised a more general method for restoring systems to a predetermined path that could be useful in the operation of both computers and cognizers. His strategy was based on the physics of dissipating free energy. Hopfield asserted that the tendency of physical systems to settle to a state of lowest energy—like coffee cooling in a mug—could be used to formulate an *energy function* approach to circuit design. He called this approach *energy relaxation.* Neural-like circuits could be built, according to the laws of energy dissipation rather than the formal laws of a computer program. Hopfield, together with circuit designers at AT&T Bell Labs and the California Institute of Technology, have designed a family of microchips harnessing his energy relaxation technique.

It has been known for a long time that any dynamic system will change in a way that minimizes its energy. This principle explains some of the striking regularities found in an otherwise chaotic world. For example, a soap bubble will wobble about chaotically when it is first formed and then settle down to a perfect spherical shape. This shape represents the lowest energy state the soap film can achieve. Hopfield described a network of nerves or a network of transistors in terms of an energy function that could serve as a blueprint for building a working model of an energy relaxation circuit. Inputs to the transistor network would push the circuit into a higher energy state, just as blowing air into a bubble increases its potential energy. The network will then slide down an *energy curve* into the nearest minimum energy configuration, just as the soap bubble will settle into a spherical shape. The state of the network at this minimum represents the result of a Hopfield computation.

Unlike the soap bubble, both nerve networks and transistor networks can be made complex enough to have a large number of different minimal configurations. This complexity makes it possible to model big problems with a large set of possible solutions, such as the long distance telephone routing done by AT&T. Hopfield went on to formulate his energy minimization strategy as one example of how collective effects can arise from physical systems.

The insight that collective effects can produce more than the sum of its parts is, in fact, a basic observation on the behavior of systems in general. Large collections of individual particles—for example the molecules in a liquid—will produce collective effects that are always the same no matter what kind of particles are used. For instance, any liquid changes into a solid as it is cooled and placed under pressure. This transition results from the large number of particles and some simple laws governing the relationships between them rather than from

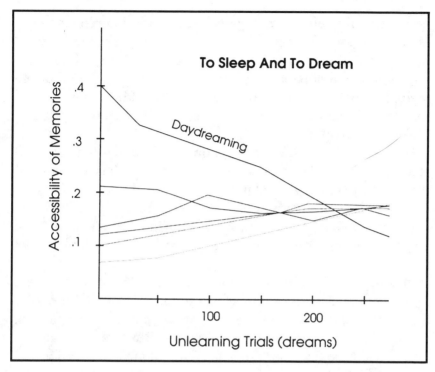

Chips that Sleep. John Hopfield noticed that his circuits had widely different access times to their various memories when used for long periods. They began to "daydream"—recall events that were spurious combinations of memories. To remedy, he put them to "sleep" so they could unlearn (dream), after which they had nearly equal access to their various memories.

their individual characteristics. The particles can be changed and the same large-scale effect will occur, but at a different temperature and pressure. It is the large numbers involved, rather than the specific details, that have the most influence over the outcome.

Another such collective effect, according to Hopfield, occurs among the large number of connections between neurons in the brain. Neurons put out dendritic trees with thousands of branches, establishing mutual connections with thousands of neighbors and communicating with all of them simultaneously. Hopfield reasoned that the overall behavior of the network may be a collective effect arising from its many interconnections. Memory, reasoning, and feeling could arise from many neural interconnections, just as temperature and pressure arise from a large collection of molecules. This theory could explain the high fault tolerance of the neural net as well. Breaking a few connections out of many is similar to losing a few molecules of a gas—the effect is negligible.

Hopfield's view could resolve a problem that has long plagued studies of the brain and nervous systems of higher animals. Although the brain is divided into rough areas that relate to different physiological functions, the finer structure has not revealed any reproducible patterns from one individual to the next. If the brain has a circuit diagram, it must involve a very loose set of specifications.

In contrast, man-made circuits are laid out on a rigorous, logical scheme that links their electrical behavior with higher level functions such as mathematical computation or rule production in artificial intelligence systems. But this strict logical link may not be necessary to achieve the complex behavior patterns of higher animals. Eventually, one may be able to trace specific high-level functions to statistical qualities of a specific collection of neurons firing. If this theory is true, the kind of deterministic lock-step techniques that people use to design computers will never apply to cognizers.

While simulating the behavior of his circuit designs, Hopfield noticed that correct conclusions were reached by computing partial results that are mutually exclusive. The method cannot be modeled with conventional digital computers. Boolean logic, which all traditional computers use, may turn out to have only tenuous links with cognizers.

To Sleep and To Dream

Because the brain has only a finite-sized repository, Hopfield reasoned that the information programmed into it must be optimized to its storage capacity. Periods of intense dreaming in sleep, many scientists agree, are when this optimization takes place. Dreams allow one to visualize things that might have happened as a result of experiences. By bringing the context of past experience to bear on new experiences, the brain is updated—leaving the familiar clear head and feeling of a new beginning one has after a good night's sleep.

Some circuits modeled on the brain have begun to exhibit a need for such periodic clearing according to Hopfield, who has observed both a need for sleep and dreams in his circuitry.

Hopfield discovered this need while building a special type of memory circuit that mimics the process of association. His so-called associative memory stored numbers as stable energy states in a network of artificial neurons. It could recall memories by association—that is, if one wanted to recall a 10-digit number, one could enter only two of the digits. These two inputs would push the network into an unstable energy state, after which it would settle into the stable state that represented the 10-digit number.

Through an investigation of two problems with this design, Hopfield discovered the significance of sleep and dreams to his cognizing circuitry. The first problem was that the memory took unequal times to recall different pieces of information. Memories recently experienced were easier to recall than those learned in the past. The more memories he programmed into the circuit, the more unequal the access times became.

The second problem was that the circuitry would volunteer information for combinations with which it had not been programmed. When presented with random inputs, the memory would produce what Hopfield called a *spurious* memory, one that had not been learned from experience, but which could have happened—a dream.

Ironically, the second problem—dreaming—solved the first problem. Hopfield maps out the states of his circuits on a three-dimensional energy surface where valleys on the surface represent stable memories. Spurious memories—dreams—are slight depressions in the surface that *were not* programmed by experience. Hopfield's version of sleep was to elevate slightly the very deep valleys in order to leave less room for spurious memories to form.

The dreams were induced by adding just a small, incremental elevation to the energy of the circuit to perturb it with associations it could have made but was not programmed to make. The net was then allowed to settle into a state of deep energy minimization, or sleep. After several sessions of sleep and dreaming, the circuits were refreshed and could once again recall all of their memories in nearly equal time.

Grossberg's Insight

While Hopfield's insight has become generally accepted, the work of Stephen Grossberg is often either revered or discounted by his colleagues. The body of work developed by Grossberg and his collaborators in some ways mirrors what one might expect from a theory of biological intelligence. It is vast, it is highly interdisiplinary and its various parts are connected in mimicry of the way brain systems communicate..

Since he proposes a comprehensive theoretical structure which could unify consciousness, psychology, neurology, biophysics, and computer science in one fell swoop, it is no wonder his work remains controversial. He has presented a theory of biological clocks with Gail Carpenter, a theory of word recognition with Gregory Stone, a theory of motor control with Daniel Bullock, a theory of conditioning with Nestor Schmajuk, and a theory of how the outer cortex integrates information with Jonathan Marshall. According to Grossberg, all these disciplines and more require the kind of unifying theory that has been enjoyed by physics since Isaac Newton's great synthesizing formulation in the 1600s. To seek this unifying theory, Grossberg founded the Center for Adaptive Systems at Boston University.

Grossberg's initial research into the history of neurology revealed that the great classical physicists had also had an interest in the subject. James Clerk Maxwell, the developer of electromagnetic theory, Wilhelm von Helmholtz, and Ernst Mach had

Stephen Grossberg. For 20 years Stephen Grossberg has been working on a comprehensive mathematical theory that describes the many levels of cognition. The Boston University professor's theories span neurobiology to psychology with mathematical precision.

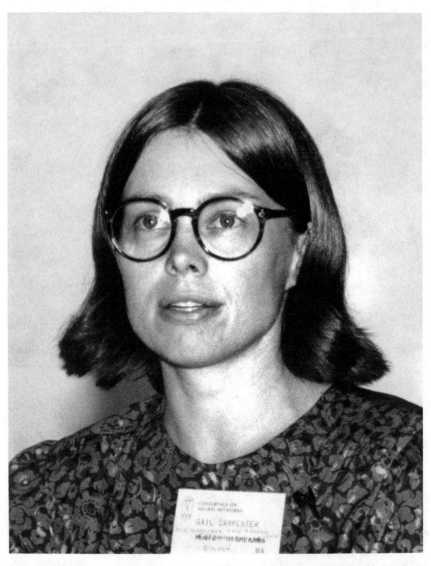

Gail Carpenter. Northeastern University professor Gail Carpenter, also at Boston University's Center for Adaptive Systems, made major contributions in the development of the adaptive resonance models. She also co-developed the Carpenter-Grossberg gated dipole concept.

all attempted to understand the workings of the mind in terms of the properties of neurons.

Though Mach lacked the mathematical tools to solve the mystery, he posed his predictions masterfully:

> The profound conviction that the foundations of science as a whole and of physics in particular, await their next great elucidations from the side of biology, and especially from the analysis of the sensations . . . psychological observation on the one side and physical observation on the other may make such progress that they will ultimately come into contact . . . [so that] a science embracing both the organic and the inorganic shall interpret the facts that are common to the two departments.   **Ernst Mach** (1914)

Mach also discovered in the retina some aspects of the mechanism of vision, but his studies did not produce any lasting effect on the development of neural science. The reason, Grossberg suggests, is that successive generations of scientists have lacked the necessary mathematical theory with which to compare the results of neurological experiments. The mathematics underlying classical physics and modern quantum mechanics has provided a common ground for experimentation. In contrast, there were no corresponding mathematical methods for comparing neurological data, and as a result, the scientists studying perception broke up into rival groups. Each group had agreed upon a theory for interpreting experimental results, but disputes as to the meaning of data would break out between different research groups. This infighting had a negative effect on any general progress in the field, since there was no way for one group to replicate the experiments of another.

In frustration, Grossberg set out to develop a unifying theory. After studying learning theory, neurology, and mathematics, he came up with a model based on associative networks that he believes is similar to neurological models of memory. Grossberg's learning theory stresses the competition among neurons for synaptic sites in the brain. He drew on cooperative/ competitive feedback mechanisms as they had been studied on a phenomenological level by Ivan Pavlov in the 1920s, by C. L.

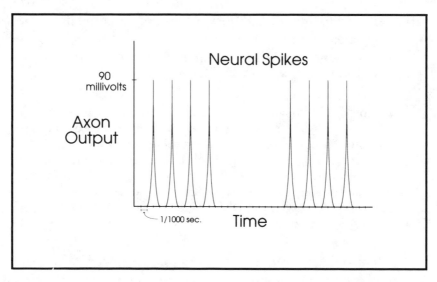

Spikes. Neural communication is done with sharp on-or-off pulses called spikes that confused early researchers into ascribing binary digital logic to the brain. Spikes come in evenly spaced bursts, because neurons must recharge for about 1/1000 sec. after firing.

Hull in the 1950s, and later in perception by F. Ratcliff in the mid-1960s.

Grossberg saw that certain characteristics of the neuron fooled early researchers into thinking the neuron was digital. Neurons have a uniform output level when *on*—about 90 milli-volts (thousandths of a volt)—and a relatively constant recharg-ing rate of about one thousandth of a second. What the digital interpretation ignored was that the information being passed from neuron to neuron is contained, not in individual firings, but in patterns of firing. Neurons often spontaneously fire indi-vidual spikes for no apparent reason and with no apparent effect. Only integrated patterns of firing produce effects.

The rapidity of a burst of spikes (the frequency) appears to carry much of the information. For example, when you pick up a hot cup, it is the increasingly rapid firing of the heat-sensing neurons in the hand that creates the sensation of heat. Random individual firings appear to carry no information whatsoever.

Neurons apparently used frequency-modulated signals to sum the information they receive in two mathematical dimensions—over the time between firing and the space of their surface area. By mapping out the relationships involved, Grossberg hoped to model their activities.

A Universal Theory?

Grossberg wanted to understand the basic functions that allow biological systems to adapt. He quickly saw that human cognition cannot be explained by one discipline. Rather an explanation must draw on mathematics, physiology, psychology, and physics. While the issues involved can be posed individually, they are in reality inextricably intertwined.

Progress in other sciences has depended on isolating a phenomenon, analyzing it, and then relating it back to the context in which it was found. This is the linear approach, and the underlying mathematics are well understood. But the various systems of the brain are inherently interrelated and must be considered together. Networks of highly-interconnected, simultaneous processes are the natural systems for representing this kind of interdependent action, but there is no simple theory that predicts the behavior of such networks.

Instead of concentrating on the analysis of an individual neuron's behavior, Grossberg set out to uncover network theories. He concluded that the computational units of adaptive behavior are distributed spatial patterns of short-term and long-term memories—not individual neuron states or memory traces. But to support such a revolutionary theory, Grossberg needed to demonstrate an alternative to the simple memory trace model that would unequivocally convince his colleges. He chose clear and distinct mathematical formulae, a method which made his writings difficult to read, but inarguably testable. He started out by gathering together the extensive data available from myriads of experiments in adaptive behavior made by Pavlov and his successors. This approach led him to a set of mathematical neural network laws that have, in turn, predicted the results of subsequent experiments.

In the early 1960s at Dartmouth, Grossberg became interested in psychology; the mechanisms underlying learning seemed particularly in need of explanation. In 1961 and 1964, he published his first papers that contained the basic differential equations describing networks that explained experiments in verbal learning. From that point forward, Grossberg dedicated the rest of his life to deriving a general set of equations that explained neural networks.

The first problem was to explain how a network could change its weights, that is learn, without becoming unstable. How can a large, apparently randomly connected network of asynchronous processors remain stable? Even more problematic, how can such networks grow and change without encountering unstable states? Even the simplest conceivable organisms have to solve this problem before they can survive and evolve into the complex nervous systems of higher animals.

Grossberg's equations eventually demonstrated that two distinct mechanisms were at work. One was associative learning, which virtually any network can achieve, and the other was co-operative/competitive interaction. In the early 1970s, Grossberg presented a set of equations that describe, in general terms, how electrical networks can be altered without becoming unstable. These equations constitute a universal theorem guaranteeing the simultaneous stability and plasticity of any nervous system, living or artificial. Hopfield's circuits follow a special case of these equations.

Clues to Stability

Grossberg's concern with stability stemmed from a growing conviction that absolute stability was the most important property of a self-organizing system. Because experience changes memory in ways that cannot be predicted in advance, a complex memory system such as the brain must maintain its own self-adjusting mechanisms to meet a changing world. These self-adjusting mechanisms must keep the body at a constant temperature in a variety of environments or mobilize fast reactions to threatening circumstances.

But all complex systems built by man so far have attained their stability only by painstaking attention to global organization principles and by constant oversight. The systems in a car work together only because of an overall engineering plan, and an intelligent mechanic must be called in whenever the plan runs across unforeseen hazards.

After much analysis, Grossberg began to formulate a way to construct large-scale, complex neural systems from locally communicating and interacting modules. The brain appears to be constructed of such modules. Clouds or pools of highly interconnected neurons receive and send signals to neighboring pools. Each of these pools has the ability to manage many different signals.

Grossberg postulated self-adjusting mechanisms that could adapt to these varying circumstances automatically. He suggested that intertwined among the other neurons were networks which keep the various subsystems operating within an appropriate dynamic range, regardless of the intensity of outside stimulation.

A neurological mechanism has been found that acts as Grossberg described. The on-center, off-surround mechanism works when neurons turn on their immediate (on-center) neighbors while turning off those surrounding the formation (off-surround). Grossberg believes this mechanism performs the global monitoring necessary to determine the optimal activity level of the brain and thus handles the automatic volume control—selective sensitivity—during pattern recognition.

The excitatory effect of an input on a neuron or group of neurons turns on centered sites, but the inhibitory effect of the off-surround turns off adjacent, excited sites. That action maintains an equilibrium over a large dynamic range by responding to input in ratios rather than in absolute terms. In other words, only a set range of excitation is allowed within the brain. Input is scaled automatically within that range by the on-center, off-surround mechanism.

For instance, when listening to loud music, the ear must turn down its volume control so low that softer sounds, such as a needle dropping, are masked out. The sound waves from the needle still reach the ear, but they cannot be heard because the ear's volume control is turned down. The range of attention can sometimes be purposefully tuned by the observer as well. One can, for instance, turn the volume up by concentrating on hearing a faint sound.

Grossberg's theory holds that the effect of any given sensation is made proportional to its environment by the on-center, off-surround mechanism. In the nineteenth century, that property of stimulus proportionality, called Weber's Law, was observed to hold throughout the living nervous system. Grossberg holds that the more recently discovered on-center, off-surround neural network is the physical means of explaining Weber's observations.

Cognizing Equations

Cognizers must perform many tasks while remaining sensitive to their environment. They must also be capable of all manner of information processing. The problem of classifying experience for the different types of information processing that must be done led Grossberg to the question of memory. A self-stabilizing system must store its memories as ratios between stimulation and background activity, since it is constantly changing its volume control. The mechanism for recording these ratios, however, was as yet undiscovered.

After much consideration, Grossberg concluded that there must be a shunting (subtracting or diverting) mechanism related to, but more sophisticated than the self-stabilization system. This proposed shunting system would siphon off some of the stimulus signal to a control mechanism that would, for instance, dilate the eye in bright light. This kind of system can maintain an equilibrium on normal levels of activity in a changing world, but the search for the kind of mathematical functions that might be at work proved long and arduous.

Grossberg began by trying the simplest of all mathematical relationships—the linear. This relationship is familiar to anyone who has ever had a bank account. The more money you put in, the larger the balance grows, and the more you take out, the smaller the balance gets. The balance varies linearly with the amount you put in or take out. However, it was quickly discovered that cognizers based on such linear math would eventually either wash out their memories to nothing or overfill to the point that memories overwhelmed each other.

From these insights arose a cooperative/competitive pattern recognition theory in which the network does information processing while maintaining no clear distinction between memory and processing. The substance of both was merely patterns of activity.

Contrast Enhancement

In Grossberg's theory, the same global capabilities—recognition with contrast enhancement—are at work in both the recognition of familiar objects and the compression of information for economical memory storage. In both of these abilities, details are picked out by virtue of a contrast enhancement mechanism. These information compression capabilities make it possible for people to store the memories of a lifetime in the same brain cells they were born with. The brain has been found to be capable of looking at a billion nodes simultaneously and picking out the one with the highest level of activity.

But storing one peak value at a time is clearly too severe a limitation on any model of what is really happening inside the brain. Rather, there must be a kind of *quenching threshold* whose level can be adjusted to determine which images go into memory and which are superfluous and can be discarded so as not to clutter up memory.

By trying out various responses modeled with non-linear

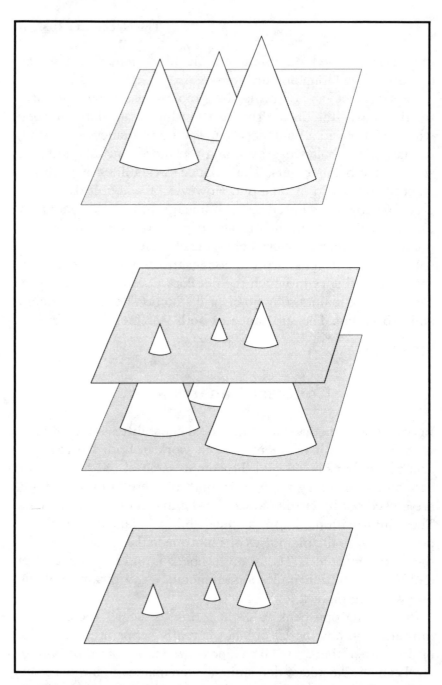

Contrast Enhancement. Grossberg claims that raw sensation (top) is contrast enhanced by virtue of a quenching threshold (middle) for compact storage of images (bottom) without degrading the ability to categorize similar future sensations in the same perceptual category.

mathematics, Grossberg found that a any of them could be mathematically proven to work, but that only one could be easily tuned-in to the current level of activity, the so-called *sigmoid*, so named because its graphically depicted response resembles the Roman " ∫."

This function is used extensively in an electronic circuitry where it is called the Schmitt trigger after its inventor Francis Schmitt, founder of the Neural Sciences Institute at MIT. A neuron modeled by a sigmoid function starts responding to stimuli slowly, then quickly picks up speed as the stimulus level rises to race across an expansive, almost linear attention span. As the stimulus level rises still further, the neuron slows its response, dropping to an asymptotic crawl at the limits of perception. This response can be depicted graphically by the symbol " ∫." By adjusting the shape of the sigmoid to be more or less steep, the response of neurons to sensations below a given level of intensity can be selectively screened out. This discrimination produces high-contrast pattern recognition combined with a rich number of memories.

Patterns that are so faint as to be below the quenching threshold are eliminated before storage can take place, whereas patterns above the threshold are contrast-enhanced and sharpened before being stored in memory. The exact shape of the sigmoid function produces a tunable filter—the attention mechanism.

This tunable filter determines what patterns will be recognized and how many details of the pattern will be stored in memory. This ability to choose certain sensations from a variety of possibilities can be achieved by adjusting the sigmoidal responses of a pool of neurons.

Conversely, lowering the quenching threshold can cause all experiences to be weighed equally. For instance, after a starting event, such as the sound of an explosion, the quenching threshold becomes very low, and everything experienced for the next few seconds is weighed and stored in memory in case it will be needed for a quick reaction. The lowered quenching threshold results in a kind of hyperattention. If nothing threatening

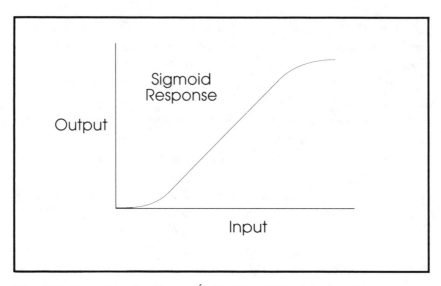

Sigmoid. Named for the Roman, ∫ , the sigmoid transfer function can accurately represent a signal while masking noise by behaving nearly linearly over most of its operating region, but sharply curtailing nearly out of bounds responses at the extreme ends of its range.

happens over the next few seconds, the quenching threshold will rise back up to whatever level was normal for the organism, and the crisis will subside.

Adaptive Resonance

While Grossberg's theories are considered speculative by other researchers, he claims to have demonstrated that associative learning is intimately combined with his tunable filter. The threshold functions of a neural network are adjusted to respond with more or less sensitivity to input signals. By adjusting its nodes to different levels in this way, a network is made more sensitive to a specific pattern of inputs—a feature of the environment, for instance. A familiar face is quickly recognized because there is a specific feature detector associated with it in memory. It takes many cognizing and recognizing events to form such a detector, but once achieved, the detector can endure for years.

Grossberg has demonstrated several such feature-detector mechanisms. A pool of neurons could be wired according to one of these mechanisms to form a programmable pattern recognizer. Another could be wired as an associative memory with learning capabilities to program the pattern recognizer. Grossberg began designing circuits that demonstrated his concept as early as 1972.

Christoph von der Marlsburg, a researcher at the Max Planck Institute in Göttingen, W. Germany, set up computer simulations that have yielded a new observation on this process. Marlsburg discovered that there is a difference between associative category learning and associative pattern learning. He found that, while tuning the sigmoid response made a network sensitive to activity levels in a signal, tuning the weights caused the network to become sensitive to categories, or codes. These codes represented prewired category recognizers, collections of related properties gleaned from experience that often came grouped together.

The significance of Marlsburg's realization was that the same network could do pattern learning and category learning in a complementary fashion. Individual patterns could be recognized and new patterns could be grouped into classes. By setting up prior categories, a network could learn to recognize particular patterns. Marlsburg's success has led the West German government to invest nearly $250 million in research that should further elucidate such cognizer construction methods.

The duality between patterns and categories was the foundation needed to develop the adaptive resonance theory. Adaptive resonance exploits this duality (between specific memories of events and the recognition categories of experience) to solve the basic problems of learning systems.

Grossberg's Big Picture

Grossberg's adaptive resonance theory brings together a grouping of theoretical insights gleaned from several diverse disciplines. Hebb's vision that the programming of the brain must be directly related to the synaptic weights contributed to the *connectionist* aspects of the adaptive resonance theory. The slowly changing synaptic weights serve as an well into which the outstanding experiences of each day can be poured.

However, the experiences of the moment are not cast in synaptic weight changes, but in the activity within a cooperative/competitive feedback net. In a network of excitatory and inhibitory signals, a resonating pattern of activity can form a standing wave. Positive feedback reinforces accurate patterns while negative feedback inhibits erroneous patterns.

Using a general nonlinear function, Grossberg has captured in

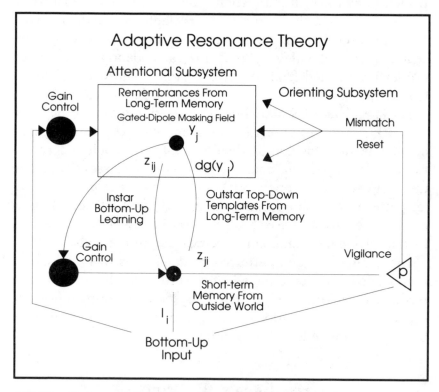

Adaptive Resonance. Stephen Grossberg's theory models short- and long-term memory. Sensation (bottom-up input) enters short-term memory—cognizing—and subsequently stimulates matching templates to come down from long-term memory—recognizing.

precise mathematical formulas how raw sensation is first scanned for patterns and then categorized by the mind into the objects of perception. His nonlinear functions use a quenching threshold to bracket attention. Below the threshold, no sensations pass to become full full-fledged perceptions. These are but fleeting color patches and wisps of emotion that flash through the mind and are lost forever. Above this threshold, contrast enhanced perceptions continuously carve out the categories of perception in the brain, beginning at birth. Outside the bounds of these categories, nothing is known, for the categories define the bounds of experience.

Kant concluded in the 1700s that the categories of perception may well define the known universe. Grossberg has come to a similar conclusion, but cast his conclusion in terms of the act of perception or measurement:

> Many of the major theoretical developments in physics have coincided with a deeper understanding of the act of measurement whereby an observer acquires knowledge about its world. Many of the results that are coming forward now can be viewed as part of the development of the universal evolutionary measurement theory in which a theory of the observer is part and parcel of a theory of an evolving world. **Stephen Grossberg** (1986)

Adaptive resonance theory is most importantly a quantitative explanation of learning and memory. It describes, in differential equations, a neural network architecture that can self-organize, self-stabilize, self-scale, and carry out self-adjusting memory searches in an arbitrary environment. Not only that, but the network can also build up a world view of categories from individual experiences that grows as it continuously self-stabilizes.

Unlike most of man's machines, an adaptively resonant network builds its own internal representations. It is not built to perform a particular purpose, but self-organizes its internal recognition categories as a function of its unique environmental experiences. Thus, it does not require a teacher or an externally supplied representation of the environment for which it was designed, as do conventional expert systems.

Adaptive resonance networks also provide an answer to van Heerdon's paradox concerning the measure of the information content in a signal. Van Heerden himself had come to the conclusion that a single objective measure of information was impossible. That conclusion motivated him to seek an information machine that could, like Grossberg's networks, seek patterns in an information channel.

Grossberg has since applied his universal theorem to a large number of empirical studies of the anatomy of the eye, experiments in learning, and studies of how the brain recognizes speech. Much of his work has been independently verified. On the other hand, psychologists have largely ignored his analysis even though it offers them a testable theoretical scheme for explaining their observations, albeit a mathematical one. Many neurologists have also ignored Grossberg's work, since they are more concerned with individual neurons than with the behavior of neural networks. But those who have come to appreciate the big picture Grossberg is pursuing have come to appreciate his far-reaching visions.

Vision a lá Grossberg

At BU's Center for Adaptive Systems, a model of vision fashioned after the adaptive resonance theory has been put together by Grossberg with the help of colleagues Michael Cohen, Ennio Mingolla, and Dejan Todorovic. This model, which proposes a cooperative/competitive hierarchy stretching from the eyes to the brain, can recognize geometric figures, even when their image is partially obscured.

The BU simulator is able to organize the continuously shaded geometric elements of a scene into perceptual groupings—sensory objects. Continuously changing textures presented the thorniest problem to the vision system, since it must decide where a boundary is to be drawn and how these boundaries are to be organized into a geometric object. In a visually noisy environment of shadows and obstacles, even simple features like a straight line must often be pieced together from incomplete line segments embedded in a matrix of irrelevant details.

It was found that a feedback loop between competitive and cooperative levels (similar to that in the eye) in a network of analog processors could cancel the noise. The competitive aspects of retinal cells have since been independently verified at the Massachusetts Institute of Technology's Center for Biological Information Processing. MIT looked at the electrical behavior of retinal cells stimulated by moving objects and found that different cells indeed responded with different levels of electrical activity for a specific direction of motion.

Grossberg's system of differential equations which describe the electrical properties of such nerve networks has also been independently supported elsewhere. For instance, an electronic simulation from Stanford University called *Spice* was used to mimic the results gleaned from frog and rabbit eye experiments. The simulation showed that an analog variant of a logical not/and- (NAND-) gate is used to organize competitive signals from different cells and register a coherent idea of motion.

Sensation Is Not Perception

What is it to actually perceive something? A flux of raw sensory data constantly assaults our senses, and only a portion of that chaos resolves into perceptions of objects. How is this perception accomplished? In ancient days it was thought that a homunculus—a little man inside our heads—reached out to a sensory object and grabbed onto it.

While this theory sounds far-fetched today, according to Grossberg the feedback mechanism among the layers of the eye in some way perform that kind of action. The eye does not send an image up to the brain. Instead the brain sends out sensing attention among the cells of the retina. Those cells, limited by their past experience, then autonomously come up with a best guess at what is impinging upon them.

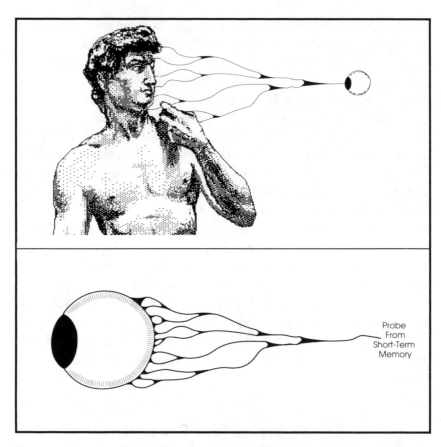

Probe
From
Short-Term
Memory

Homunculus. Ancient philosophers thought that vision was the result of a homunculus that reached out to the object and grasped onto it (top). Some scientists today think that theory was not as far fetched as it sounds. No "little men" are inside the head sending out nets to catch sensation. Instead of reaching out to the object, the homunculus reads the light patterns that impinge upon the eye. The back of the eye is coated with narrow cells (rods and cones) that feed a hierarchy of ganglia a million strong, providing a rich variety of pathways for homunculi (bottom). Like a police radar unit that reads reflected radar signals, the reflections of the probe are interpreted by the brain as the objects of perception.

The fact that neurons grow excited relatively slowly and maintain the excited level for a short time after stimulation has been experienced by any one who has ever touched a hot stove. It takes a second for the burning sensation to become a clear perception, and even after you pull your hand away, the pain continues for a few seconds.

Though they were devoid of technology, the ancients clearly understood these basic truths. Perhaps these obvious and enduring truths transcend time, for whether in philosophical treatises or Hollywood's films, today's continual speculation on the future of technology contains the same basic understanding.

How Does It Do It?

There are about 100 million retinal rods cells in the eye continuously sending information to the brain. This much information would overflow the largest computer memory or the brain in very little time.

Luckily the vast amount of information that these cells continuously gather does not have to be stored away by the brain. The eye reaches out to the object instead, according to Grossberg, with several hierarchical layers of cells which narrow down and interpret a continuous stream of information.

The raw data is treated as a continuous stream from which patterns can be extracted by association. As the senses take in information, they cause it to vibrate against a background of sympathetic resonances wrought from encoded memories of similar past experiences. The raw sense data combined with the associations from the past then resonate forward and backward in the mind until a coherent image forms, whereupon the conscious mind is notified. In the conscious mind, both current recognized patterns and a mixture of associations from past experiences congeal into emotional opinions enforced by hormones and subsequently acted out.

This act of resonance is similar to what happens in a piano or other stringed instrument when one string vibrates sympathetically in response to a sound of a certain pitch. The eye learns a variety of visual categories, constantly conditioning them by new experiences. Each category then sympathetically resonates whenever a similar sensation impinges from the external world.

The thing that resonates is thought by Grossberg to be a cloud of neurons—an interconnected group of cells surrounded by inter-neurons (smaller simpler neurons) that together form a feedback system which resonates in response to particular classes of sensation. As a string vibrates because its reflecting energy runs back and forth along the wire—physical feedback— a neuron cloud creates a similar resonance with electrochemical feedback. In a cognizer, the feedback is electronic.

Outstar Learning Theorem

One of the most controversial aspects of Grossberg's theory of perception is his support of a model of the brain where perception is the result of an outward-reaching homunculus. His outstar learning theorem, developed in the 1960s, guarantees that any pattern can be learned by an outstar sampling signal—a homunculus.

The first step in the process of perception, according to the theorem as applied to vision, is to project a pattern of sensation onto the cells at the back of the retina. According to Grossberg's theorem, the outstar network then sends a sampling signal— the homunculus—to the retinal ganglia cells. The outstar cells in the ganglia layer then reach out and sample the bare sensation from over 50 different types of feature-extracting receptors on the retina.

The sampling signal perturbs the retinal cells and returns a pattern of signals, each one of which is proportional to the intensity of activity at that cell. The sampling signal is sent out as a probe, so to speak. Then the measured reflection determines the degree of conformance—how much the two match. Each retinal cell gets a sampling signal and returns one that is proportional to its current activity level when compared to the sample. The pattern of returned signals measured by the outstar neuron cloud is the frontier boundary between raw sensation and conscious perception.

Given this model, the outstar learning theorem says that the relative synaptic weights converge to the average value of the pattern that was caused by raw sensation. The outstar learning theorem gives rise to a model of perception that is not only quantified with equations, but that also agrees with the phenomenological experience of the world.

People acquire the categories of experience from the patterns

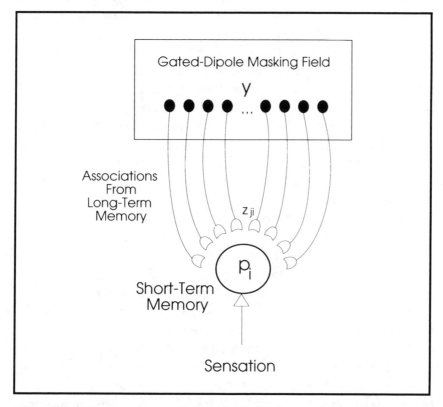

Short-Term Memory. According to Stephen Grossberg, short-term memory is a mixture of impressions from raw sensation combined with myriad associations from long-term memory. The experience of "now" is a resonating associating mixture of the two.

among sensations. These patterns are captured internally in a resonating neuron cloud whose feedback responds to patterns as they are experienced. Thus the elements of one's ongoing experience of the world are a set of short-term memories whose physical counterparts are resonating neuron clouds.

The functional unit of short-term memory is a resonating pattern which fades in about 15 seconds if not committed to long-term memory by association with existing memories. These are the fleeting experiences of daily life.

The functional unit of long-term memory is a spatial pattern of synaptic weights. These slow changing patterns are constantly updated. They are also the categories of experience because they provide the sampling signals that probe our current sensations for patterns they have seen before.

Learning itself is the process of transforming those short-term patterns to long-term category codes that can later be used for the stimulus sampling of sensation to yield new instances of perceptions. The reflected sampling signal helps form the categories of perception. And those categories help to construct more refined sampling signals with which to perceive the world.

If resonances are cognized often enough, they will be committed to long-term memory and become a candidate for future associations with the sampling signals that evoke memories. The repeated perceptions eventually become the categories of experience itself.

Memory recall, under this theory, is similar to perception. Rather than sending a sampling signal to the receiving cells to sense patterns in the environment, the brain sends a performance signal to long-term memory cells. The reflected energy is then measured and averaged in order to resolve the response from these categories into known patterns, just as in perception.

This probed readout of the long-term memory's synaptic patterns is allowed into short-term memory where it can contribute to the experiences of the day. Thus the phenomenological experience of the day is a combination of patterns currently being received and associated patterns from memories of the past.

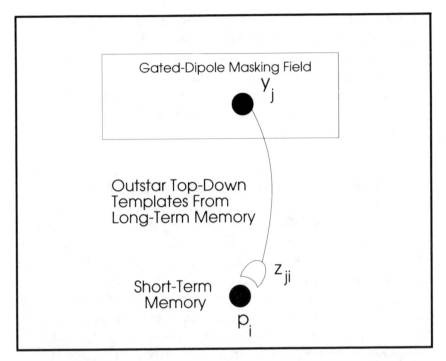

Long-Term Memory. Synaptic weights (Zij) hold long-term memories, according to Grossberg. His outstar learning theorem holds that templates, contrast enhanced composite images, are stimulated to come down into short-term memory by association.

Memories can be jogged by their similarity with current sensation, but the jogging mechanism is a stimulus into long-term memory. Just as perception is built from sensation with a homunculus stimulus signal, accumulated knowledge is retrieved from long-term memory with a similar signal.

Many phenomenological aspects of the world are also explained by the outstar model—the fact that the intensity of an experience controls the rate of learning, for instance. Sufficiently shocking events will create sensations shocking enough to be perceived so strongly as to be never forgotten. The outstar learning model also explains the old proverb: *practice makes perfect.* Each time a perception is formed, either from sensation or by recalling from memory, the patterns it contains will be reinforced in long-term memory. The more it is perceived or pondered, the better it will be remembered.

The outstar learning theorem is a universal learning device that can be used to describe and build systems for many types of cognitive functions. It spans an area from learning based on prior experience to motor control to encoding temporal order spatially inside the brain.

Instar Category Development Theorem

The companion to the outstar learning theorem is the instar category-development theorem. The instar model explains how the categories of experience are derived from patterns of sensation and continually updated while remaining stable.

The various outstar networks, in the eye and other senses, reach out to raw sensation in order to cognize patterns competitively until a particular pattern or feature congeals. The more persistent these features are, the more strongly they affect long-term memory.

The instar coding theorem predicts that these long-term memories will be attuned to certain patterns effectively acting as feature detectors. The first time a perception is made, it is cognized. When it is remembered, it is cognized again—recognized—in the conscious mind. The instar coding theorem guarantees that these feature detectors will recognize features whose patterns have similar characteristics. As such, these detectors can serve as the basis for an internal classification system—the categories of mind.

A particular array of feature detectors, honed fine by experience and repeated practice, serve to define the limits of perception. Raw sensation comes in and is preprocessed into a field of vision, sound and other sense categories. That field of sensation forms a pattern in short-term memory. The intensities of the various nodes in this pattern reflect the intensities of the features being perceived in the external scene.

The short term pattern of activity then works its way through a series of levels where long-term memories adjust their adaptive weights in response to the new short-term memories. Persistent short-term patterns will make long-term changes deep in the system, while fleeting short-term perceptions are soon washed out of memory.

In other models, learning must be terminated after a finite number of trials since further training will cause only ceaseless recoding of categories, especially in the face of novel new input. Rival learning mechanism models cannot attain stability unless the lessons of new experience are ignored. But the adaptive-resonance model provides the stabilization necessary through the complementary outstar and instar theorems. The outstar gathers coherent patterns from the external world and impresses them on long-term memory. These long-term memories then become the templates of experience, and the instar theorem guarantees that they will be able to identify correctly similar patterns.

Then, by selectively filtering experience for the already familiar and the truly novel, stabilization is achieved. The adaptive resonance model stabilizes learning in ceaselessly novel environments by using its categories or templates to filter experience. This process stabilizes the learning experience regardless of how arbitrary the patterns' processes may become. Novelty is always perceived against a de-emphasized background of the familiar.

Once a category of representation has been activated at a high level, it can send stored patterns relating known features of that category back to short-term memory. Ordinary consciousness is the reception of inputs from the environment and from the stored knowledge of long-term memory according to the stimulated categories. For instance, in a game of cards, the particular hand being played serves as the raw sensation. As the pattern of the hand is scanned, long-term memory feature-detectors find combinations in it that are recalled as being good. Our conscious experience is one of a pattern-matching game between the novelty perceived in the cards and the known patterns from long-term memory.

The process is stabilized by the complementary stimulation

received back from long-term memory. Once the proper categories are stimulated and recognized, long-term memory sends back to short-term memory its accumulated knowledge of those features, thus stabilizing present experiences with memories of the past. If the category returned from long-term memory does not match the present short-term memory state, thanks to a quickly changing scene or simply a mistake, for instance, then the feature detectors are quickly reset by an orienting signal to clear the head and try again.

Patterns registered from the external world form arbitrarily. However, people can attune their pattern detectors to expect certain patterns, such as waiting for a phone call or for the tea pot to boil. Sometimes feature detectors can be attuned so sharply that they misinterpret ambiguous cues as the anticipated cue: "Did I just hear the phone ring in the other room?" These top-down patterns from long-term memory prime the system for quick responses, such as when waiting for the starting gun, the classroom bell or the 5 P.M. whistle.

How can the conscious individual tell the difference between patterns that originate from long-term memory and signals from features detected in the external world? The answer is in the attention mechanism. The attention mechanism switches between external world and long-term memory, fixing on the one that is the most active at the moment. The result is either cognizing (sensation plus attention) or recognizing (long-term memory plus attention). The third combination (sensation plus long-term memories) happens only when the attention mechanism's automatic-gain control is turned way down, such as during daydreaming. Otherwise attention is turned either inward or outward.

When attention is fixed on an activity, such as reading a book, the automatic gain control is turned down so that spurious patterns from sensation are ignored. Even though a radio is playing or people are talking in the background, one can continue reading because the attention mechanism is primed for the matches between long-term memory and short-term memories that may be stimulated by the act of reading.

Vigilance Rule

A key parameter in adaptive resonance theory is vigilance. Vigilance sets the level of mismatch between a particular template from long-term memory and current perceptions from the outside world. If a mismatch occurs, then a reset wave is sent to the orienting subsystem.

Low vigilance leads to a situation where mismatches are widely tolerated, such as during daydreaming, when even dissimilar objects can be placed in the same rough categories. High levels of vigilance, on the other hand, lead to very fine categorical sorting of environmental stimuli, such as during the scrutinizing of a suspect bill.

In either case, the top-down templates from long-term memory eventually stabilize the coding process and settle on a internal representation that categorizes familiar experience. The fineness of the chosen categories is proportional to the current vigilance level.

Gated Dipoles

While simple electronic models of neurons, especially the threshold gate models, have been very good at mimicking the underlying mechanisms of learning and memory, they do not easily show the emotional side of neural behavior. To simulate the mechanisms of emotion, the action of chemicals on the behavior of neurons must also be included in the model.

Chemical reactions are fundamental to neural function. It is a chemical imbalance between the interior of the cell and the external brain fluid that creates the electrical impulses the neuron uses to communicate. When the neuron fires, the chemical components separated by the cell membrane are allowed to mix. This mixing process generates the electricity underlying our mental world. The chemical imbalance must be restored if the neuron is going to go on sending signals.

The chemical imbalance is restored by an ion pump that separates positively and negatively charged ions. But the ion pump can work only so fast. At times, a neuron will fire so frequently and so long that the ion pump's efforts cannot maintain the required chemical charges. The neuron then becomes exhausted and stops firing, although it may still be receiving signals from its neighbors at a level that would normally cause it to send signals.

Purely electronic neural models do not have this capacity for exhaustion. Neural circuitry uses traditional power sources that are, for all practical purposes, inexhaustible. There are valid engineering reasons for using such power supplies—they greatly simplify the task of circuit design, for instance—but they do not provide an accurate model of neurons in the brain.

It might be said that evolution employs accidents of nature as design principles. One of the accidents of nature that neural systems have found useful is the difference between the speed of electrical signals and the speed of chemical reactions. In general terms, it is the tension between the time scales of electrical and chemical processes, interdependently functioning inside people's heads, that produce emotions. In order to fully simulate a neuron, an electronic model must simulate these chemical processes.

This role of chemical reactions was developed by Carpenter and Grossberg. They found that many functions in the nervous system could be reduced to a circuit module which they called a *gated dipole*, a module which encompasses the chemical transmission of signals between neighboring neurons. One peculiarity of the gated dipole was an additional response that occurred briefly when input to the module was cut off. This cutoff response set Grossberg to thinking about some of the unsolved problems of the nervous system.

This unusual output response is a result of the depletion over time of *neurotransmitter* in the gated dipole. If the input to a gated dipole suddenly increases, the output will also increase. If the input remains at a higher than normal level for any length of time, the output will slowly drop off as the supply of neurotransmitter in the simulated synapse is depleted. If the input signal drops back to normal, the output will drop below normal until the supply replenishes itself.

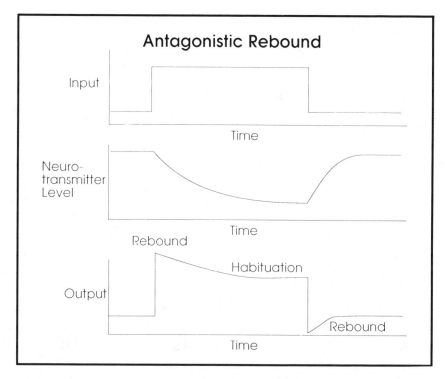

Neurotransmitter. The synapse's neurotransmitter multiplies inputs (top) to get an output (bottom). But the neurotransmitter is depleted while an input is present (middle). When an input first comes on the output over-shoots, but slowly habituates to a steady state. When the input goes off the output under-shoots until the neurotransmitter is replenished.

This mechanism may explain the symptoms of drug tolerance and withdrawal. When a drug is introduced into the system, it forces a response from the brain that tails off with time as important transmitter chemicals are depleted. If the drug is suddenly removed, the brain's output drops back below normal levels—withdrawal—until the supplies of chemicals can be replenished.

Of all the processes in the brain, the chemical ones are probably the most difficult to model accurately in electronics. While an understanding of these mechanisms is necessary to the construction of full-fledged cognizers, much work can be done with simpler models that do not include chemistry.

5

Learning to Learn

Last Piece to the Brain's Puzzle

The difference between the capabilities of current computers and man is, to a large extent, the ability to learn. But learning is the least understood domain of cognitive science. As such, it represents the final frontier to cracking the mystery of the brain.

A functional understanding of the learning process holds the promise of endowing cognizers with a thoroughly inquisitive nature. By building in an ability to learn that is modeled on man's own, cognizers could transform artificially intelligent (AI) expert systems into genuine synthetic intelligence.

Anyone who has ever had to describe software or computer programming to a layman can appreciate that these concepts are very difficult to explain. One reason for the difficulty is that these concepts have no straightforward analogy in the world. Nature has evolved a substitute for programming called learning. Learning allows every living thing to adapt to its environment without the sort of preconceived categories that are implicit in a computer program.

Even artificially intelligent (AI) programs, such as expert systems, do not learn. The best they can do is house a body of knowledge in their memories and provide a convenient, human-like way of retrieving it. Even the smartest computers today are only pretending to be intelligent, because they can not learn without a human expert and a computer programmer.

The ability to learn represents a fundamentally new hurdle for technological development, because even the most complex machines made today are too rigid to learn. Men have designed machines—from toaster oven to hydroelectric dam to industrial robot—to act in precisely determined ways. The computer, like the rest, works the way it does because its program has been carefully planned to follow rigidly controlled pathways. Any tendency toward unforeseen behavior in machines is ruthlessly suppressed. Even if the unplanned-for behavior is better adapted to a problem, owners of such unstable machines nevertheless have the error eradicated.

As living beings, however, we have all experienced and adapted to unpredictability in nature. Natural systems have developed an alternative to lock-step determinism in order to deal with a world which abounds in unforeseen events.

Learning is not essential to cognition. Many species of lower intelligence get along quite nicely without significant learning abilities by virtue of behavior patterns built into their genetic blueprints. But any creature that must deal with an environment disturbed by novelty, from primordial shellfish to dinosaurs to men, must possess learning mechanisms in order to survive.

The job of the machine designer has traditionally been to find ways to control and eradicate any errant behavior, whether it is well adapted to the situation or not. Any novel behavior on the part of a machine is suppressed for fear of losing control. Thus, machines that learn have been forbidden to exist by virtue of accepted technological design principles. Learning, on the other hand, means amassing knowledge of novel events. When one learns something new, the brain's inner workings have changed in an unforeseen way. Situations that one never expected or imagined are somehow tamed, not by changing the situation, but by changing the brain. The

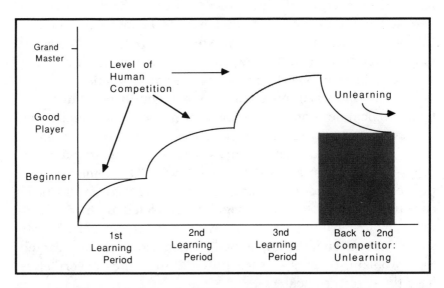

Computer Chess. A chess playing computer that learns from its opponents must face the problem of regressing against less admirable foes. Here it increases its skill level for each of the first three games against increasingly skilled opponents. But when the learning machine faces a less skillful opponent, it regresses by learning the bad moves as well as the good.

construction of learning machines therefore requires a new technology free of rigid determinism.

As the complexity of modern machinery increases, control becomes more of a problem, simply because there are more ways that a machine can break down. If the mind in all its intricacies is also a mechanism, it must have some additional organizing principles that technologists do not yet fully understand. While people are capable of highly organized and rigidly determined behavior, they are often at their best when behaving in unantici-pated, eccentric ways—playing games, entertaining fantastic notions or learning something new.

Learning represents such a paradoxical process that very little has been discovered about how the brain accomplishes this feat. Learning obviously requires memory, since it implies, by defini-tion, the ability to build on prior knowledge. But effective learn-ing also requires other cognitive mechanisms, such as a sense of aesthetics or discrimination. There is a chess-playing program that has reached a new level of complexity in computer learning. As the program plays against better and better opponents, it becomes more and more sophisticated. After achieving a certain level of sophistication, however, the program can lose its accom-plishments by playing against a bad player. It goes on blindly learning the poor chess player's habits, not "realizing" that this particular opponent is not up to its standard of excellence.

Expert systems represent an excellent way to conceptualize problems for consideration by users. They allow known facts and a train of reasoning to be stated explicitly, usually as a series of *If-Then* rules such as:

"If a man is over 65, then there is a 70% probability that he is retired."

These kinds of rules and facts can be amassed in an expert system in order to achieve a fixed level of artificial intelligence. But once these systems have risen to a certain level of machine "understanding," they remain there. They incorporate no mech-anism by which they can learn from the environment on their own. This fact is not surprising, since the mechanism used by expert systems to build their knowledge base is not readily

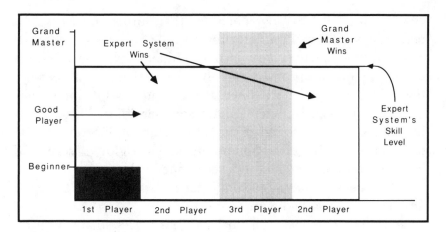

Expert Chess System. Chess playing computers that do not learn, expert systems, will win or lose in strict proportion to their skill level. They hold their level of "intelligence" constant, hence their ability to win a match can be calibrated against an opponent's skill level and the outcome reliably foretold in advance.

adaptable to learning. The world does not present its lessons in simple *If-Then* fashion.

Thirty years of *computer engineering* has revealed that logic can make computers that seldom err. *Cognizer engineering,* though, may show us why the human animal must sometimes err. After all, trial-and-error depends upon error to foster learning.

Computer memories have an impressive ability to recall an enormous amount of detailed information without any errors. But this ability to remember is not accompanied by the kind of adaptability represented by the ability to learn. Having electronic access to everything that is known is of little use, since all that is required at any time is the one fact that applies to the present circumstances. Without the ability to distinguish what is relevant to a given problem, a computer will simply take longer to sift through a larger mass of information in order to find what is appropriate.

Computer designers are now coming to recognize this lack of discrimination as a practical problem. Computer data pools have grown to the point that the central processing unit (CPU) cannot search through the masses of data in a reasonable amount of time. Searching mechanisms must recognize the relevance of the information they seek in order to retrieve it in a timely fashion. Inaccessible information is useless, even though it might be entirely accurate. Information network designers have now begun to structure data by building the logical relations among its constituent parts into the memory structure itself.

Although human memory retrieval is less accurate than its electronic counterpart, it is more effective because it is integrated with learning. The information absorbed in a lifetime of experiences can not be recalled at will, but the relevant memories can be brought to the surface when they are triggered by present thoughts. This ability to associate current circumstances with all of one's accumulated experiences simultaneously is the brain's way of learning.

The ability to learn seems both simpler and more mysterious than man's other faculties, and philosophers, psychologists and neurologists have all attempted to understand its underlying mechanisms. Theorists maintain that if all psychological phenomena are physical processes in the brain, then obviously learning causes some physical change in the brain. But the exact location where those changes occur has proven elusive.

Mistaken Notions

The question of where memories are stored led René Descartes, the great seventeenth-century philosopher, to suppose that the brain was the repository of memories, each one of which left a *trace* on the substance of the brain. Descartes' memory traces were renamed *engrams* by the twentieth-century French scientist, Richard Sermon.

In the late 1940s, a Canadian brain surgeon, Wilder Penfield, discovered that if he touched electrodes to various areas of the brain of conscious patients, the patients would experience memories—hear and see things that had happened in the past. By stimulating the same area of the brain, Penfield could reproduce

145

the same memory again and again. He thought he had finally found the engrams. Other researchers began duplicating Penfield's work in animals with astounding success.

Separately, an American researcher, Karl Lashley, devoted thirty years of his life, from 1920 to 1950, to the search for engrams. But Lashley's experimental techniques turned out to be too crude to unlock the fine detail of memory. He also chose experimental methods that had embedded within them many different variables. For instance, Lashley had rats run mazes, and then searched their brains for the exact spots where the engrams of what they had learned were stored. Unfortunately, rats use many different strategies to solve mazes, so that no single mechanism was found. In the end, Lashley concluded that engrams evidently were not to be found. He speculated that memory must somehow be distributed rather than located at individual sites. This insight is Lashley's lasting contribution to neural network theory.

But the truth of Lashley's speculations was not recognized immediately. Many other researchers throughout the 1950s attempted to use more refined techniques to succeed where he had failed. One group at the University of California at Berkeley,

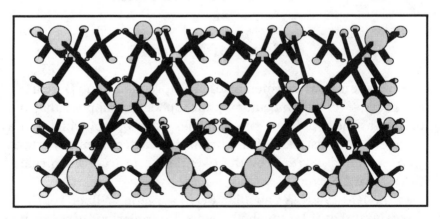

Memory Molecule. Twentieth-century scientists at first searched for specific molecules that allegedly contained a code enabling experiences to be stored and remembered. No such molecule has ever been found. Instead genetics was found, but alas it is fixed for life.

including David Krech, Mark Rosenzweig, Edward Bennett, and Marian Diamond, selected pairs of newborn rats that were as similar as possible and isolated them, providing one with a stimulating environment, the other with a very dull environment. Their assumption was that those animals with the stimulating environment would learn more. After nearly three weeks, autopsies were performed on both rats' brains, and the group was able to show conclusively that the neurons' growth is affected by learning. Not only did a rat raised in the stimulating environment have a heavier cortex, but the individual cells of its cortex appeared to be larger.

These verified findings stimulated a barrage of studies searching for a memory mechanism inside the neuron cells themselves. Some scientists reasoned that the larger cells must be storing memory in the form of molecular codes in neural chemicals. The most likely candidate for this *memory molecule* was thought to be ribonucleic acid (RNA). Studies made by the Swedish scientists Holger Hyden and Jan-Efrik Edstrom in the early 1960s were able to confirm that there was more RNA in neurons than in any other cell. Further studies by Hyden even seemed to indicate that as learning took place, more and more RNA accumulated in the neuron.

However, extremely small quantities of RNA accumulated in neurons with more training. The cells themselves were much larger than could be accounted for by mere RNA accumulation. This fact stimulated other studies attempting to show that protein was the memory molecule, with several early reports of progress in this area. For instance, graduate students James McConnell and Robert Thompson went so far as to chop up trained worms and feed them to untrained worms, claiming that learning was transferred by the ingestion of smart protein. Most of these studies, however, have subsequently been discredited and the search for the memory molecule abandoned.

While reductionist scientists searched for the atoms of memory *inside* neurons, one psychologist at McGill University, Donald Hebb, correctly supposed that it was not the neurons themselves, but the connections between them that stored memories.

Empirical evidence had shown that brain cells die daily and are seldom replaced. If neurons contained encapsulated bits of knowledge, say of one's grandmother, then the death of those neurons would erase the memory of one's grandmother. Clearly that is not the case. Hebb's pioneering book *The Organization of Behavior* (John Wiley, 1949) resolved this mystery by postulating that chemicals in the synaptic connections *between* neurons were modified by nervous activity during learning. In the brain, where neurons link up, we have already seen how the electrical activity of a sending neuron stimulates chemical changes that produce electrical activity on a receiving neuron. Hebb's postulate was that these electrochemical connections between neurons were strengthened by repeated use.

More precisely, Hebb suggested that an increase in the electrical activity at a synapse naturally increased the capacity of that synapse to produce neurotransmitters. Just as a muscle grows

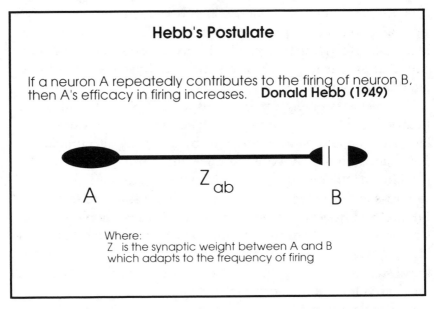

Hebb's Postulate

If a neuron A repeatedly contributes to the firing of neuron B, then A's efficacy in firing increases. **Donald Hebb (1949)**

$$Z_{ab}$$

A   B

Where:
Z is the synaptic weight between A and B which adapts to the frequency of firing

Hebb's Postulate. Donald Hebb correctly identified the mechanism of memory. Put simply, the more a synapse fires, the bigger its effect (its "efficacy"). But this so-called "synaptic weight" is not Descartes' illusive "trace," since memory is distributed within the network.

larger when exercised, synaptic connections grow stronger when they are used often. The experiences of the external world cause nervous activity which strengthens the connections between the neurons stimulated and results in learning. Learning leaves the memory of events behind as *synaptic efficacies*—the tendency of neurons to fire in similar patterns.

Altering the connections within a neuron network alters the way the network responds to new stimuli. Thus its behavior would change with new experiences—it could learn. The set of synaptic *weights* so formed, Hebb reasoned, could represent the accumulated knowledge of the network's past experience all at the same time. But the question remained: does this alteration result in true learning?

Hebb had suggested how the brain could store new memories as the result of learning, but it took many years of follow-up studies to confirm his findings. Subsequent researchers have discovered that memory formation as a result of learning is more complex than Hebb originally supposed. Nevertheless, his original insight continues to serve as the starting point for all modern neural network theories.

First Recorded Cognizers

Hebb's ideas exerted a strong influence on high school classmates Frank Rosenblatt and Marvin Minsky, who separately tackled the problem of building synthetic networks that functioned like the brain. Minsky built a full-blown hardware simulator in 1951 with tubes and mechanical servos. Rosenblatt attacked the mathematical side of Hebb's idea, summarizing his findings in his book *Principles of Neurodynamics* (1962). In this book, Rosenblatt transformed Hebb's ideas about the brain into machine design principles for a visual pattern recognition system that became known as the *perceptron*.

Rosenblatt took Hebb's qualitative postulate regarding synaptic modifications and quantified it as a learning mechanism for machines. His *perceptron convergence procedure* described a

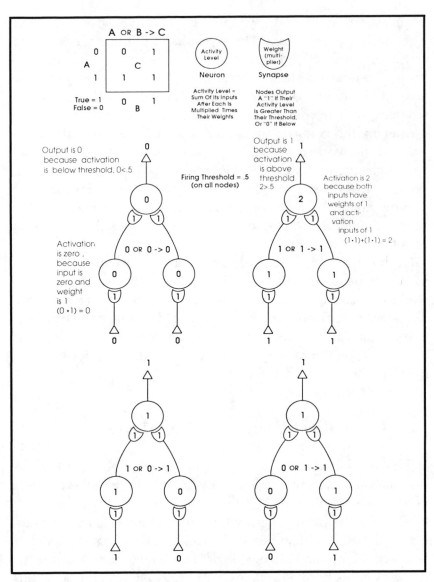

OR. A simple two-layer perceptron can perform logical functions like the OR operation here. A neuron's activity level is the sum of its inputs from other neurons after each is multiplied by its weight. If the sum exceeds the neuron's threshold (here .5), then it sends a "1" to the next neuron. If the sum is less than the threshold, then the neuron sends a "0" to the next neuron.

very general method for systematically modifying the connections in an artificial neural network—what we now call a cognizer—to elicit whatever behavior was desired from it. While Rosenblatt suggested some concrete ways to implement his general procedure, he left it to other researchers to come up with particular procedures for specific applications.

Despite its generality—and in some ways because of it—Rosenblatt's perceptron concealed within it the seeds for many derivative neural-based architectures which germinated in the subsequent years. The perceptron, in its simplest configuration, consists of two layers of artificial neurons, or nodes. The input layer accepts patterns from the outside world while the output layer supplies results to the outside world. The strength of the connections between the two layers—the weights—are determined by a teacher who modifies them, one at a time, until the desired mapping between input and output is obtained.

In addition to a practical version of Hebb's ideas about learning, Rosenblatt's perceptron theory also includes the *threshold* concept, originally proposed in 1943 by Warren McCulloch and Walter Pitts. A linear model of neurons would have them merely sum their inputs and send that sum onto the next node, but McCulloch and Pitts added a nonlinearity by comparing that sum to a preset threshold. If the sum is over the threshold, a signal of unit strength (1) is sent on to other nodes.

A perceptron can easily be wired to simulate many logical relations. A logical OR outputs *true* (symbolized by a logical *1*), whenever one or both of its inputs is true. For example, say the statement *A or B* is *Either Smith owns a Ford or Brown is in Barcelona.* If Brown happens to be in Barcelona, then *A or B* is true. If Smith owns his Ford and Brown is in Barcelona, then *A or B* is still true. The only time it is false is if both of its subpropositions are false.

An electronic device that simulates this relationship will have two inputs, each of which can be a *0* (false) or a *1* (true). The device will have one output. If either of its two inputs are *1*, or if both are *1*, then the device will output a *1*. Otherwise, it will output a *O*. The illustration (page 150) shows how a two-level cognizer can be set up like such a simulator.

Perceptron's Criticized

Even though the perceptron could be shown to solve logical problems very similar to those on which the digital computer is based, its popularity was short lived. In 1969 Marvin Minsky and Seymour Papert released their book *Perceptrons*, charging that simple, two-layer networks had strict limitations that made them inferior to digital computers. Rosenblatt's perceptrons had been intended as general machines that researchers could adapt to their specific needs. Minsky and Papert constructed many such specific versions of two-layer perceptrons and delineated the classes of problems that each could solve. Their critical appraisal, while entirely accurate, nevertheless ran counter to Rosenblatt's speculation about the uses to which simple perceptrons could be put. As a result, Minsky and Paper's criticism deflected researchers from work on neural networks to developing artificial intelligence on standard digital computers.

Though Minsky and Papert's specific criticisms were manifold, a simple example has become their hallmark. Minsky and Papert correctly demonstrated that a two-layer perceptron with three artificial neurons was incapable of learning a particular logical relation called the *exclusive-OR*. The exclusive-OR, in contrast to the normal OR holds that if both inputs are true, then the output should be false. An example is: *Either Smith owns a Ford, or he owns a Chevy*. If Smith owns one or the other of the cars, then this statement is true. If he owns neither of the cars, then the statement is false. With exclusive OR, if he owns both cars, then the statement is false. Unfortunately, there is no way to wire a two-layer perceptron with three units to correctly decode all four of these combinations.

This limitation is overcome either by adding a third layer of nodes or by introducing feedback. (All information in a normal perceptron flows from input to output, a "feed-forward"

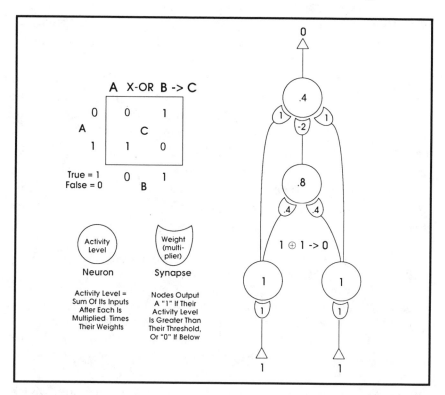

Exclusive-OR. By adding just a single intermediary neuron, the three layer perceptron can then perform the exclusive-OR operation. Here only the "difficult" case of $1 \oplus 1 \rightarrow 0$ is shown. The threshold is set at .5 here, forcing the output node below threshold $(1 + 1 - 1.6 = .4)$.

arrangement.) In the 1988 Epilogue to *Perceptrons*, Minsky and Papert objected to this characterization, claiming that multiple layers of nodes cause an impractical explosion in the number of nodes required for large problems. They also say that feedback is objectionable because it adds an element of sequential processing that leads to overly-long learning sessions.

Nevertheless, both of these extensions of the perceptron will work. A multilayer perceptron, trained by feedback, can be made to learn any possible logical relation. It is easy to come up with simple examples to prove that multilayer perceptrons can perform logical operations as easily as digital microchips. The advantage of cognizers built from such perceptron circuits is that they learn the logical relations needed for an application from experience. Digital systems, on the other hand, must be explicitly engineered to perform each particular task.

Rosenblatt united Hebb's synaptic weight idea and McCulloch and Pitts' threshold concept in a set of designs for a machine that could learn from experience. The perceptron could be trained to modify its connection strengths by being presented with sample input/output pairs. But Rosenblatt was so enamored of the perceptron's capabilities that he began to claim it could handle more complicated transformations than the digital computer. Rosenblatt's biggest mistake, perhaps, was to claim too much for his idea.

> . . . the perceptron has established, beyond doubt, the feasibility and principle of non-human systems which may embody human cognitive functions at a level far beyond that which can be achieved through present day automatons [that is, the digital computer] **Frank Rosenblatt**, *Principles of Neurodynamics*, 1962.

Such bold assertions about the superiority of perceptrons led directly to Minsky's criticism in *Perceptrons:* "I now believe the book [*Perceptrons*] was overkill . . . [I was] irritated with Rosenblatt for over claiming and diverting all those people along a false path . . ."—Marvin Minsky, interview with *The New Yorker*, Dec. 1981.

Rosenblatt led the fledgling electronics industry to believe that the perceptron represented a fundamental breakthrough in artificial intelligence (AI). In fact, he had discovered only one simple learning mechanism. Minsky and Papert's treatise pointed out the obvious limitations of such simple perceptrons, convincing AI researchers that writing software for digital computer would be more fruitful than repairing the flaws in the perceptron. For nearly two decades, funding merely trickled into cognizer research. Except for some small isolated projects in the United States, Japan, and Europe, research into building machines similar to the brain all but stopped.

Rosenblatt's overly-optimistic claims demonstrated the danger of promoting simplified models of perception and cognition as universal answers to the problems of building artificial

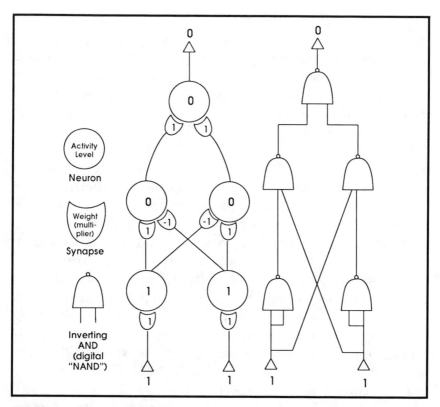

NAND. The three-layer perceptron bears an uncanny resemblance to an array of standard digital NANDs (devices called "gates" that perform an AND operation before taking the complement or NOT of the result—hence NAND from NOT-AND). But unlike digital circuitry which must be reconfigured for each problem, the perceptron can learn any logical relation without having to be re-wired.

intelligence. Because of the perceptron's failure, AI research has been held back immeasurably by being shackled to the sequential digital computer. Cognizers are now regaining that lost ground by emulating the simultaneous use of multitudes of neurons in the brain.

The Perceptron's Ills

The perceptron was shown by Rosenblatt to be able to learn from experience, just as the real neural networks of the brain do. Unfortunately, neither Rosenblatt nor any subsequent researchers have been able to demonstrate a guaranteed method for finding the appropriate synaptic weights for any particular problem within a specific number of training sessions. Many learning rules have been developed to train multilayer perceptrons and other cognizer designs, but none of these rules is the universal solution sought by AI researchers.

Throughout the 1970s, AI researchers sought the *general problem solver* or GPS as a best method for solving problems with digital computers and AI software. Even the best efforts of these general problem solvers, however, resulted in only a shallow understanding of any given problem. The next step taken by AI researchers was to add domain specific knowledge to a GPS, spawning the motto *in the knowledge lies the power*. Throughout the 1980s, context specific rules about the domain of knowledge associated with a given problem were added to general problem solvers. The result is today's expert systems—AI software being used in applications as diverse as medical diagnosis and oil well exploration. Expert systems continue to be successful in domains where there is a body of clearly defined knowledge. For instance, interviews with experts in medical diagnosis can produce a large number of rules and facts that can be incorporated in turn into an expert system. An intelligent query system enables novice users to access this knowledge.

Expert systems have been successful in restricted domains, but they have come nowhere near their original goal of producing a general problem solver. In Minsky and Papert's words:

> . . . the most successful applications of AI research gain much of their practical power from applying specific knowledge to specific domains. Perhaps that work has now moved too far toward ignoring general theoretical considerations, but by now we have learned to be skeptical about the practical power of unrestrained generality, (Epilogue to 1988 edition of *Perceptrons*).

While cognizers will probably fare no better as general problem solvers, they do hold out the promise of easing the development of specific problem solvers, because they can learn. An AI system must be explicitly programmed by a knowledge engineer after human experts in a domain have been interviewed. But there are many ways for a cognizer to learn specific problem solutions by example. There will never be a single cognizer that can solve all problems, but there is probably no specific problem that one cannot build a cognizer to solve.

This lack of a universal learning rule should not discourage researchers from searching for specific learning rules for particular problems, and that is precisely what researchers have been doing in the years since the perceptron's disgrace. There now exist a multitude of learning rules that specify how to train multilayer perceptrons and other cognizers to perform useful tasks in particular cases.

Connectionism

Since the search for learning rules was essentially an attempt to discover how to adjust the synaptic weights associated with each connection, the movement came to be called *connectionism*. The connectionists maintain that the connections in a neural net hold the code that controls mental activity in both brains and cognizers. Not all researchers who study synaptic modification are called connectionists, but those whose heritage is the perceptron usually are.

Rather than locate each element of knowledge in a single artificial neuron, connectionist machines distribute knowledge in a pattern in the network. A remarkable result is that similar patterns allow the machines to generalize—these machines can face new situations and come up with workable solutions derived from their prior experiences. The intuitive reason for this generalizing behavior is that a connectionist model is detecting the regularity in its own knowledge. That regularity is detected because knowledge for connectionist machines is more than just facts: it also includes the relationships among facts. Rules-of-thumb can be derived from the inherent regularity in these relationships.

The major stumbling block to connectionism has been that the internal representations of a learning machine—connection

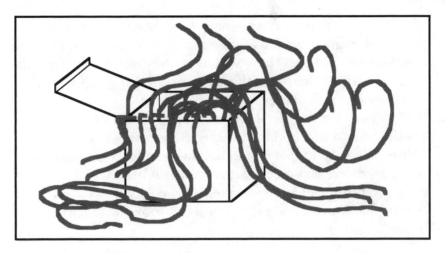

Connectionist Glop. Early connectionists could build learning machines, but they had no underlying theory to interpret how their machines wired themselves. Dissection only got the researchers "connectionist glop" that was no easier to decipher than brain tissue.

topology and associated synaptic weights—are often incomprehensible. No analytic method has been devised to specify just what connection topology and weight values will result in what behavior. Since cognizer theory was inspired by biophysical studies of nerve networks in animals, it seemed logical that an autopsy could be used to find out exactly how specific learning rules solved problems. Learning machines were taught to solve simple problems such as adding two numbers, after which the machines were dissected to find out how the internal synaptic weights were configured. The result was usually *connectionist glop*, as Carnegie-Mellon University's David Toretzky puts it. Apparently it is as difficult to derive an analytic understanding of machine learning by dissection as it is to discover how a living brain works by dissection.

Curing the Perceptron

While no universal method for determining the proper connections and associated weights for a cognizer has been found, many specific methods have been devised to allow a machine to learn a suitable set of weights for a particular problem. Work in this area began shortly after Rosenblatt publicized his work in the late 1950s, (prior even to his 1962 book.) A pioneer in this field was Bernard Widrow, who in 1960 transformed the learning rule Rosenblatt derived from Hebb into a working model for machine design. The learning rule Rosenblatt proposed was a general procedure intended to spawn particular rules for specific applications. The engineering approach of Widrow and his student, Ted Hoff, resulted in a learning mechanism that has proven effective in many real-world circumstances.

Although cognizer designers do not have an analytic method for determining the correct weights for a neural network in advance, they can, in effect, reward beneficial trials and punish erroneous ones. Specifically, the Widrow-Hoff learning system derives an error signal by comparing the observed performance of a neural network to the desired performance. This error signal—the gap between the actual response and the desired response—is used to strengthen or weaken trial connection weights and thereby control the learning process. This mechanism has been proven effective for several practical applications—such as adaptive-equalization filtering in all high-speed modems (computer-to-computer communications devices) and adaptive echo-cancelling for an increasing number of two-way satellite communications links.

A simple Hebbian learning rule strengthens connections whenever they are used, even if the machine has learned its task perfectly. The Widrow-Hoff rule maintains that no weight change should be made if no error is detected between the real performance and the desired performance. If there is a discrepancy between the real and desired results, then the amount by which the connection's strength is changed is made proportional to the magnitude of the error. The Widrow-Hoff rule, successful as it has been, still does not provide an analytic method for determining the weights before hand, but it does provide a means of training individual cognizers to perform specific tasks.

Other researchers have come up with even simpler alternatives to the perceptron learning rule. For instance, in 1974 Teuvo

Teuvo Kohonen. Helsinki University of Technology professor Teuvo Kohonen has stunned speech researchers with self-organizing neural network designs that can quickly and accurately recognize Finnish. Asahi Chemical is casting his work in microchips for Japanese.

Kohonen used a simplified version of Rosenblatt's work in his design of an associative memory that learns from a teacher. Associative memories are modeled on the way human memory works. Unlike a digital computer's memory, in which each bit of information is stored and accessed through an address (like a mailbox address), an associative memory stores related data in groups and is capable of recalling all of the data in a group when presented with any part of it. If the contents of Kohonen's associative memory were names and telephone numbers, then submitting the first name to the memory would cause it to recall the complete name and the telephone number.

Kohonen, like Rosenblatt, used just two layers of artificial neurons. But unlike Rosenblatt, Kohonen left out the McCulloch-and-Pitts threshold function, which had made the perceptron a *nonlinear* system. This omission made Kohonen's associative memory very easy to analyze, but limited the number of patterns it could learn.

In Kohonen's system, the first layer of artificial neurons accepted inputs from the environment while the second layer produced outputs that were stimulated both by the inputs and by a training signal. During the learning phase, each connection between the input and the output was strengthened in proportion to the amount of input activity times the training signal. After learning, the training input was removed so that the output nodes were stimulated solely by the input units.

Kohonen and others have modified various aspects of the simple linear associative memory to build systems that easily learn orthogonal patterns. For instance, in 1977, James Anderson built an associative memory in which he constrained his networks to form their connections along the edges of an imaginary box—his *brain-in-a-box* design. The artificial neurons were at the box's vertices and connected to each other along the edges.

Back Propagation of Errors

The researchers mentioned above showed that, in simpler versions of the two-layer perceptron, a teacher could assist the learning process through a training signal connected to the output layer. Other researchers have sought to transcend the limitations of a simple, two-layer perceptron and harness the full capabilities of a multilayer cognizer. The basic approach these theorists used was to add feedback connections—connections that feed error information back from higher levels to lower levels while the cognizer is learning its tasks. While cognizers normally feed information forward from input layers, allowing them to feed error information backwards from output to input can speed the learning process. This technique was introduced by Widrow, but it has been fully developed for multilayer threshold networks by others.

The first such multilayer network was the reduced coulomb energy network (RCE), introduced in 1980 by Nobel laureate Leon Cooper and his Brown University department chairman, Professor Charles Elbaum. Through many alterations and refinements of a multilayer derivative of the perceptron model, Cooper and Elbaum have developed a network device that can reliably solve real world problems. It was patented in 1982 and is currently at work on a variety of problems for Ford Motor Co., General Electric, Chemical Bank, and other well-known corporations.

An RCE neural network is composed of three layers of artificial neurons tied together by variably weighted connections, with the signals sent from one layer to the next multiplied by these weights. The pattern of interconnections determines the network's capabilities, but changing the weights allows it to learn a particular application. The RCE network itself performs *category learning,* that is it learns to classify patterns presented to it into preset categories. Unlike other neural networks, an RCE-based system automatically adds new artificial neurons as learning progresses to keep the network at an appropriate size for the problem at hand. After its training, the RCE neural network can automatically generalize—that is it can correctly classify new patterns into existing categories.

For example, RCE neural networks are being used to read handwritten documents in the United States, Japan, and Europe. The categories the network learns are the characters of the alphabet,

Leon Cooper. He won the Nobel prize for co-authoring a theory of superconductivity, but shortly after winning, shifted his work at Brown University to
neural networks. Cooper is now chairman of the first public neural network
companies, Nestor.

and training consists of presenting various handwriting examples to the network. Once it is trained on the handwriting samples, it can then generalize to classify properly new examples from people whose handwriting was not a part of the training set.

When a novel pattern is presented to a working RCE neural network, the output node that corresponds most closely to a trained category fires. The internal layer maps the inputs to the proper output(s.) If only one output fires, then the network is said to classify unambiguously the input. But, if more than one output fires, then the results are ambiguous. To resolve ambiguities, new feature types (the crossed $\emptyset$ used by science writers) and new categories (foreign alphabets) can be added to an RCE neural network without retraining the system on what it has already learned. In practice, multiple RCE neural networks, each of which is expert at some patterns but inexpert at others, are combined with domain-specific rules that supervise the overall activities of the system.

Though the RCE neural network was independently developed, it was introduced the same year that a relatively unknown graduate student first introduced the similar *back propagation of errors* technique. In 1980, Paul Werbos demonstrated the feasibility of back propagation in his Ph.D. dissertation in applied mathematics at Harvard University. But his demonstration went relatively unnoticed until it was independently redeveloped in 1982 by David Parker at Stanford.

Parker's work came to the attention of David Rumelhart (University of California) at San Diego and James McClelland (Carnegie-Mellon University). Those two, together with what they call the PDP research group, have gone on to refine and popularize the Parker and Werbos technique.*

*For more information see *Parallel Distributed Processing,* MIT Press, 1987. The PDP research group consists of Chisato Asanuma (Salk Institute, San Diego, Calif.), Francis Crick (Salk Institute), Jeffrey Elman (Univ. of Calif., San Diego), Geoffrey Hinton (Carnegie-Mellon University), Michael Jordan (Univ. of Mass., Amherst, Mass.), Alan Kawamoto (Carnegie-Mellon), Paul Munro (Univ. of Pittsburgh), Donald Norman (Univ. of Calif, San Diego), Daniel Rabin (Intellicorp, Mountain View, Calif.), Terrance Sejnowski (Johns Hopkins University), Paul Smolensky (Univ. of Colo.), Gregory Stone (Boston Univ.), Ronald Williams (Univ. of Calif., San Diego), and David Zipser (Univ. of Calif., San Diego.)

Rumelhart and McClelland saw that the perceptron's problem was in its lack of internal representation—it had no third internal or hidden layer, a fact which meant that it had to rely on the similarities provided by the external world. Whenever the outside world provided few or no similarities between patterns—such as with the exclusive-OR that groups (0,0) with (1,1)—a network without an internal representation is unable to perform the mapping between inputs and outputs necessary to recognize all conceivable patterns.

With the addition of a single, internal layer with which to identify those natural dissimilarities, a perceptron could be made to recognize any set of patterns. Rumelhart and McClelland have not been able to derive a general learning rule that will solve all problems with a third layer of hidden units within a specified amount of time and with a network whose size can be determined in advance. Nevertheless, they have demonstrated how three layer perceptrons can indeed solve nearly all types of logical problems in a specific domain.

Rumelhart and McClelland's version of back propagation uses a learning rule that is derived from the Widrow-Hoff rule, also called the Δ-*rule*. Their broader interpretation of the Widrow-Hoff rule, known as the *generalized Δ-rule*, enables errors to be propagated backwards from the output layer to the internal layer and on to the input layer. This kind of cognizer requires connections that go forward as well as backwards among the layers of artificial neurons. Several new issues are raised by the forward and backward connection topology, such as whether the connections should be matched—connections in either direction having identical weights—or separate.

The generalized Δ-rule uses an input pattern and a random set of initial weights to produce an output, which it then compares to the desired output or target. If there is a difference, then the weights are changed to reduce the difference. With no hidden units, the generalized Δ-rule reverts to the standard Widrow-Hoff rule, but with hidden layers, back propagation of errors can be used to train each layer in turn. Once the desired output is produced for each input in the training set, then learning is turned off and the cognizer deployed for testing with novel patterns.

This procedure generally converges upon a pattern of proper synaptic weights. Sometimes, however, it can become fixated in errors that no weight change can eliminate. In that case, the cognizer's weights are reset and training begins anew. The generalized Δ-rule for back propagation has shown that the limitations of the original perceptron were vastly over estimated in the 1960s.

Boltzmann Machine

While Rumelhart and McClelland trained their networks with a deterministic method, (back propagation) two other members of the PDP group went on to develop a learning procedure that instead uses *stochastic*, or random, methods. In 1984, Geoffrey Hinton (University of Toronto), and Terrance Sejnowski (Johns Hopkins University), developed the Boltzmann machine using the statistical randomizing methods made famous by the physicist Ludwig Boltzmann. They begin with a fixed number of artificial neurons and connections, and add weights to the connections through their learning procedure until the network's performance is adequate for the task at hand.

The Boltzmann machine uses binary nodes that take on the values *0* or *1*. In a manner similar to back-propagation cognizers, these nodes are arranged as an input layer, an output layer, and a middle *hidden* layer isolated from the real world. The connections in the Boltzmann machine are symmetric; that is, there are two connections between each artificial neuron, one going to and one coming from, both having identical weights.

Most perceptron models merely add up their inputs and then use complex, nonlinear functions to determine their outputs. The Boltzmann machine does just the opposite. It does not have an output function per se—nodes simply output their activation value. Instead, the Boltzmann machine uses a very complex stochastic input function to determine the activation value.

This input function is the most novel aspect of the Boltzmann machine. The function is not a deterministic mapping, but a probability function. If an artificial neuron has many positive inputs, then there is a high probability that it will fire. If it has a lot of negative inputs, then it has a low probability of firing. There is, however, no simple, one-to-one mapping between inputs and outputs.

Learning in the Boltzmann machine proceeds in two phases. First, patterns are randomly presented to the visible units using a simple Hebbian learning rule—the more a given neuron fires, the more likely it is to fire. In the second phase of learning, the system is allowed to run for a period with no inputs. Because the input function is stochastic, some of the input neurons will continue to fire even though there is no outside stimulus. During this phase, an anti-Hebbian rule is used—neurons that fire often become less likely to fire. Intuitively, the system works because during the first phase, network activity results from both the environment and the connection matrix. But during the free running phase, only the connections are at work. The anti-Hebbian learning rule subtracts out the effect of the connections themselves, leaving only the effect of the environment.

Cooperative-Competitive Cognizer

The connectionists' researchers, while greatly expanding the design of Hebb, McCulloch, and Pitts, still have their roots in the original perceptron. Others, however, have been attempting to model more recent physiological discoveries as well as provide suggestions to biologists as to where further investigations might be fruitful. One of the most successful of those groups is the cooperative-competitive theorists.

While the connectionists were working out the details of back propagating errors, the cooperative-competitive theorists were incorporating the tendency of aggregates of neurons to use an on-center, off-surround topology. That is, when a given neuron is

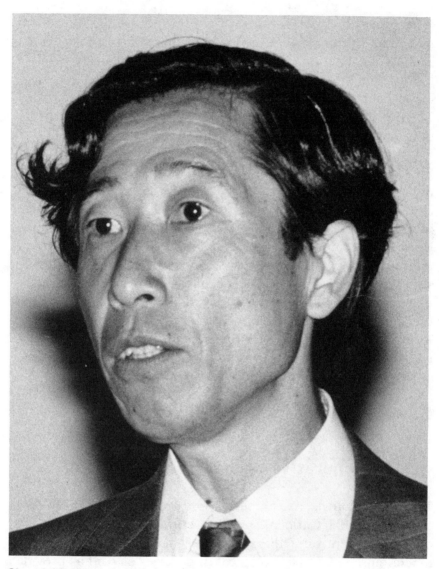

Shun-ichi Amari. University of Tokyo professor Shun-ichi Amari is a long-time neural-network mathematician. Amari has reconciled cooperation with competitiveness within networks of nerve cells. He has written two books (as yet untranslated) and is co-editor-in-chief of *Neural Networks* magazine.

Kunihiko Fukushima. The foremost Japanese cognizer researcher is NHK Laboratories' Kunihiko Fukushima. His cognitron and the second generation neocognitron have honed the crowning perfection of Frank Rosenblatt's perceptron over the last 20 years.

excited, the neurons around it tend to be inhibited by different neurotransmitter chemicals.

Cognizers built on this principle learn a unique, internal representation of the outside world without supervision—they have no teacher or preset group of features by which they classify their input. Cooperative-competitive networks start off with a set of nodes that are identical except for some randomly distributed parameter that makes each node's operation slightly different. Learning then allows units to compete for the right to respond to a given subset of inputs, thus making them feature detectors.

Various other versions of competitive-cooperative networks have been designed by Boston University professor Stephen Grossberg, University of California professor Michael Arbib, University of Tokyo professor Shun-ichi Amari, Max Planck Institute (West Germany) professor Christoph von der Malsburg, and researcher Kunihiko Fukushima at NHK Laboratories (Tokyo).

6

Neural Circuitry

Forerunners of the Cognizer

Though studies of neurons will likely reveal further unexpected results in the future, technological advances need not wait. In fact, the most successful cognizer circuitry so far has not been that which accurately modeled neurons, but that which worked well with current technologies.

In many ways, modeling neurons with microchip circuitry takes electronic technology back to basics. Digital circuitry has been successful to the detriment of the kind of microchips needed for cognizers—analog microchips. While analog circuitry has been used in high-fidelity music reproduction equipment, even that arena is switching to digital circuits with the advent of digital signal processors (DSPs), compact disks (CDs), and digital audio tape (DAT). The construction of a cognizer, though, requires analog circuitry. Thinking, it appears, is a continuous or analog and not a digital process.

Microchip technology was designed to model George Boole's propositional calculus, which was based on the logical values— true and false. Boole believed that these two values were all that were needed to describe completely the human thought process. True and false were easily represented in electronic circuitry with the two information values, 1s and 0s. The use of only two values to represent all data was the guiding principle behind the reduction of computer circuitry to digital microchips. This reduction greatly simplified circuit-design efforts and provided a simple model for developing silicon-integrated circuits (ICs)— the digital microchip.

The brain's activities are known to use analog, electrochemical systems to achieve thought. The neurons communicate among themselves, not with digital 1s and 0s, but with voltage spikes that stimulate the production of chemical transmitters. As more spikes arrive at a synapse in a given amount of time, the synapse releases more neurotransmitters. The released chemicals stimulate a specific neuron located near the synapse which then begins to increase the frequency with which it sends voltage spikes to its synapses, and so on. Rather than sending messages coded in some digital symbolism, the neurons emit chains of voltage spikes that increase in frequency as urgency increases, causing an avalanche of chemicals to rain down across the synaptic junction.

The chemical transmitters released at the synapse add another level of complexity to this signal-transmission model. Different kinds of neurotransmitters will have different effects on a neighboring neuron. Some transmitters are excitatory, making it easier for the neuron to fire. Others will inhibit the neuron, causing it to recede from voltage-spike generation. Still others can make the neuron numb so that it does not feel the effect of its other inputs. These and many more such responses form a complex, nonlinear structure out of which arises the behavior of real neural networks.

Researchers are far from unraveling the intricacies of the chemical transmitter system. One study at Harvard University has identified over 50 distinct neurotransmitters in the neural networks of the retina. Staining techniques show that each of these transmitters is associated with a specific type of interconnection pattern between neurons.

The chemical transmitter system also provides a variable time base for the nervous system. Chemical reaction rates are very much slower than those of electrical signal transmission, which introduces an additional flexibility into the timing operations of biological neural networks not present in digital systems. For example, synapses take time to replenish their supplies of neurotransmitters. This time lag results in a type of short-term memory in biological neural networks—a chemical imprint on the system that fades with time. High levels of activity at a synapse deplete the synapse's chemical supply, lessening its response to strong signals—a form of chemical normalization.

The fact that the firing of a neuron is an all-or-nothing spike seems to support the digital explanation of how the mind really works. In digital systems, all signals are rigidly timed by a clock signal. A digital circuit will not operate unless all signals and switching events in the circuit are carefully synchronized to that clock. Like the lever on a manual calculator, the clock tick marks the performance of each operation. All current computers, from mainframe to desktop personal computer, are based on this common digital foundation.

Not long after the first digital computers appeared, some visionary circuit designers saw a way to take advantage of the electrochemical aspects of neural behavior to replace the serial clock. The adaptability and plasticity of real neural circuits could be imitated with wires and transistors. Although these alternate approaches to circuit design enjoyed a short vogue during the 1960s, they had practically all died out by the mid-1970s. Still, these early efforts provided important inspiration for today's neural circuit designers.

Memistor

One of the first approaches to an electronic model of the neuron was an adaptive-circuit theory pioneered by Bernard Widrow in the early 1960s. Widrow began his quest for neural nets when he took his doctorate at MIT in 1956. That summer, after Widrow had become an MIT assistant professor, he attended a summer-long AI conference at Dartmouth College that turned his attention to machine intelligence.

After thinking about machine intelligence for six months, Widrow decided to adapt neural techniques to signal processing, though he did not label himself a neural researcher. He named his learning algorithm *adaptive-signal processing*, and today his seminal adaptive-filter technique is used in many industries.

His earliest work is recorded only on internal MIT reports, but his first paper on the subject of adaptive systems appeared in 1959. It described sampled data systems—a form of digital signal processing—that could adapt to the signals they tracked. Like artificial neurons, adaptive filters have many weighted inputs to a summing node. At MIT, Widrow worked on a simple model of a neuron for pattern recognition and signal processing.

175

By adding a threshold-detecting device on the output, Dick Mattson, then a graduate student at MIT, helped create the adaptive-linear neuron (Adaline) in 1959. Like the perceptron, the Adaline was a threshold-controlled summing node. For reasons of convenience, Adaline's binary output was encoded as either +1 or −1, +1 if the weighted sum of the inputs exceeded a threshold, and − 1 if it did not. When many of these units were used at once, the result was called *multi-Adaline* or *Madaline*.

Shortly after developing the Adaline, and after a short stay at MIT's Lincoln Labs, Widrow made the transition to Stanford University. There he continued to work on adaptive filters, concentrating in particular on methods of adjusting the input weights. Working with Ted Hoff, a graduate student, he eventually found that by graphing the least mean-square error (a statistical measure) as a function of the weights, they could calculate

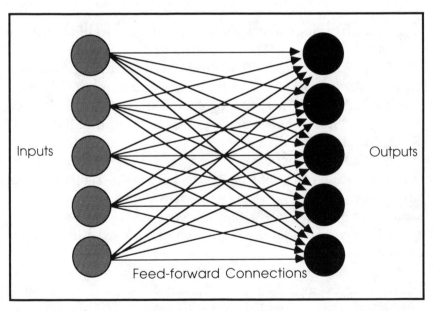

Inputs

Outputs

Feed-forward Connections

Perceptron. Frank Rosenblatt's pioneering perceptron used a simple feed-forward network in which each connection was from an input to an output. The learning mechanism assigned values to the connections, called weights, to solve a number of perceptual problems.

the optimal weights for a given problem. This technique, later known as the Widrow-Hoff rule, was used to calculate the weights for the Adaline.

While the Adaline's capabilities were impressive, its initial applications were limited because each neuron required an operator to adjust its weights. Widrow and Hoff realized that the Adaline should be able to change its weight electrochemically like a neuron's synapse—act as a resistive analog memory. Hoff implemented the concept by submerging carbon rods the size of pencil leads in test tubes of a plating solution (sulfuric acid and copper sulfate). As the rods became electroplated, their resistance changed. A control wire in the tube adjusted the degree of copperplating, making the test tube a three-terminal memistor cell—two terminals attached to the rod and one to control the amount of electroplating.

Commercial versions of the Memistor are still sold, but the advent of inexpensive semiconductor technologies has made them largely obsolete. Hoff, like so many other talented electrical engineers, dropped out of neural research and plunged into digital design shortly after leaving Stanford. He is subsequently credited with inventing the microprocessor in the early 1970s.

Neuristor

Another approach to emerge from Stanford's laboratories at the same time as the memistor was a device called the *neuristor*. It was invented by H. D. Crane, a graduate student who described the device in his Ph.D. thesis in 1960. That thesis became a blueprint for subsequent neural systems, the theory of which has slowly developed over the following two decades.

The motivation behind the neuristor was to find a new way of transmitting electric charge without diminishing the signal. Electrical energy dissipates as it travels through wires, largely because the wire is passive. Neurons, on the other hand, have found an effective means of transmitting electrical signals with little or no dissipation. According to Crane, they can do this because unlike passive wires, they actively generate electrical energy as they transmit it.

The basic neuristor copies this method of undiminished signal transmission, allowing any number of connections to be made among the neuristors. In technical jargon, these connections are referred to as *infinite* fan-out, rather than a fan-out of just five or six as for digital devices. Crane reasoned that an infinite fan-out could make possible very large, realistically sized, synthetic neural networks having an inherently high level of interconnectivity.

Modern microelectronic design techniques were applied to the basic neuristor concept to create devices that manipulated packets of charge. These charge packets are analogous to the voltage spikes generated by neurons. R. W. Newcomb has shown that a consistent analog computing technique is possible using devices of this type. He also showed that real neural networks could be modeled with these neuristor-based devices.

A prototype chip based on this approach, but using more

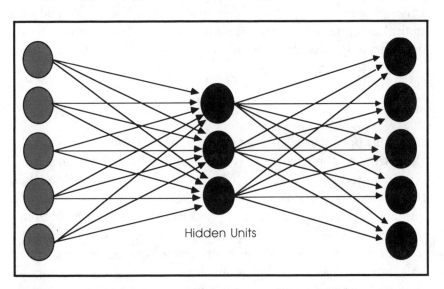

Hidden Units

Hidden Units. Connectionists improved upon Rosenblatt's original perceptron by adding so-called "hidden units." By adding more layers between the input and output, hidden units, the circuit could be adjusted to learn input/output pairs that the perceptron could not.

advanced semiconductor technologies, was demonstrated at the University of Maryland's Microsystems Laboratory. The circuits on the chip directly emulate the frequency coding of signals found in living neurons. Newcomb, working with Nevine El-Leithy, used modern device innovations to add even more realism to the chip. A new type of memory cell, the floating gate, can store a small amount of charge indefinitely and was used in a whole new generation of memory chips and programmable circuits. Newcomb and El-Leithy used floating gates to store and release charge packets of different size, just as synapses release more or less chemical transmitter in response to voltage spikes. Like Widrow-Hoff's memistor, Newcomb and El-Leithy's floating gates could store memories in a continuous, analog medium—synaptic weights. The result is that neural-type microsystems acquire some of the plasticity of real neural networks.

In Chapter 4, we saw how the perceptron gave rise to the connectionist circuit-design movement. Connectionist researchers have so far had mixed success at realizing their designs in hardware. Some, such as Rumelhart and McClelland, have designed multilayer versions of the original perceptron using hidden units. Others, such as Teuvo Kohonen, have managed to produce working, practical circuits. A variation of Kohonen's two-level neural network has been used in a *talking typewriter* that replaces the keyboard with a microphone.

The main criticism leveled against the connectionist approach is that while the method used for calculating the weights is easily executed as an algorithm on a digital computer, there is no known circuitry in the brain to which it corresponds. The issue is not important if effective learning algorithms are the only goal of the research. But many theoreticians feel that the first objective of cognizer research is to find a way to produce cheap, effective circuitry that imitates the real behavior of neurons. To achieve that goal, neural behavior must be modeled accurately and in great detail. Many important and resourceful organizations are seeking that very objective with the latest electronic design and process methods.

AT&T Goes Back to Basics

Always in the forefront of developing technologies, AT&T's Bell Laboratories—the inventors of the transistor—are doing pioneering work on neural microchips. A group of Bell Lab's biophysicists has been collaborating with electronic engineers on the development of cognizing circuitry.

This research group first developed a circuit modeled on the learning functions of the Limax garden slug. Slugs are a popular creature for neural network studies because they have very large nerves that can be easily studied. They also have around only 20,000 neurons, few enough that they can all be cataloged. The Bell Lab's group has been compiling a database that details the quirks of each of the Limax's neurons. When completed, this database will be a milestone in neural network research—the first time that an entire nervous system has been cataloged.

The Bell Lab's group has built a model that incorporates some of the lessons learned from studying Limax, both in its natural state and in computer simulations. The simplified model uses four neurons to represent the slug's taste buds that are connected to an auto-associative memory similar to the one

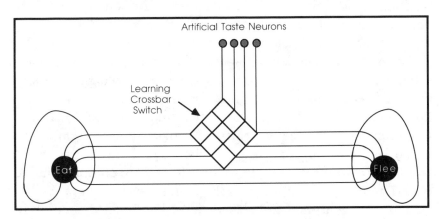

Limax Maximus. A research group that combines the study of living organisms with electronic circuitry at Bell Laboratories was inspired by the garden slug *Limax maximus*. The circuit shown explains classical learning experiments by Pavlov involving the sense of taste.

designed by John Hopfield, who has been consulting with AT&T for several years.

The memory grid in the Limax circuit makes associations by coasting to an energy minimum—a stable state that represents a solution to the problem the slug faces. Once a minimum has been reached, the circuit sends signals to the motor neurons, causing the slug to either flee from or eat the food it is tasting. The same solution can be reached by different paths. In fact, the researcher who set up the simulated slug often cannot give a precise account of events during its operation.

While the Limax model was simple and elegant, AT&T felt it needed a better understanding of the fundamental underpinnings of neurological science. Accordingly, it has set up joint projects involving specialists in mathematics, computer science, physiology, and psychology. These projects include everything from experimentation on live laboratory animals to the construction of custom microchips.

Frankenstein's Time Arrives

The methods AT&T uses for etching tiny features on microchips are now being retooled for nerve-cell farming. Tiny barriers are built in a 10-micron-wide silicon chip that is then flooded with liquid nutrient. These nutrient filled chips form a sort of neural rice paddy into which severed nerve cells (also from a slug) can be transplanted, fed, and studied. Once transplanted, these nerve cells immediately begin growing new connections to one another. AT&T hopes that by studying the way these neurons form and use their interconnections, synthetic versions of neural nets—cognizers—can be built.

This method of constructing organisms on chips is not envisioned as a means of building living cognizers but as a means of studying neurons and their interactions, particularly how neurons change the electrical conductivity of their connections. These changes in conductivity are thought by AT&T researchers to be one of the unplumbed, yet primary means of programming the brain. An understanding of the macroscopic behavior of the neurons is also desired, but learning how the connections use calcium and other chemicals to alter their conductivity is the immediate goal.

Small but Complex

Individually, neurons appear to be much more complex than once thought. While it was once believed that neurons represented single bits, AT&T experimental results have demonstrated that neurons are at least as complex as the kind of microcomputer used in a hand-held calculator. Several experiments at AT&T have shown that single neurons can handle the kind of signal-processing functions typical of the microprocessor systems used by engineers to control machinery.

For instance, one neuron studied at AT&T—also from a variety of garden slug—clearly has the job of attenuating the signal—turning down the volume—between two other neurons when activity gets above a certain threshold level. A microprocessor performing that function would have to monitor constantly the amount of electrical activity between the two neurons, summing it over time. When the processor measured a buildup of activity that exceeded a preset threshold, it would attenuate the signals by adjusting the electrical resistance of the connection between the neurons. A neuron performs this function by chemically changing the conductivity of the connections between the two other neurons when activity exceeds its threshold.

Neurons also use time and distance in their operations, factors that are viewed as a barrier to faster computation in digital circuits. Some neurons use a time delay in a feedback circuit as a means of storing memories or as a unit of time for calculating rates of change. The point at which a signal enters a neuron can also be used to derive values needed in a function the neuron is performing.

Hopfield's Theory Cast in Silicon

John Hopfield has also been enlisted by AT&T to help build cognizing circuits. In Chapter 4, we examined Hopfield's energy-minimization theory in which neural networks maintain a state of lowest energy. When new inputs raise these networks to a higher energy level, the networks settle back to a

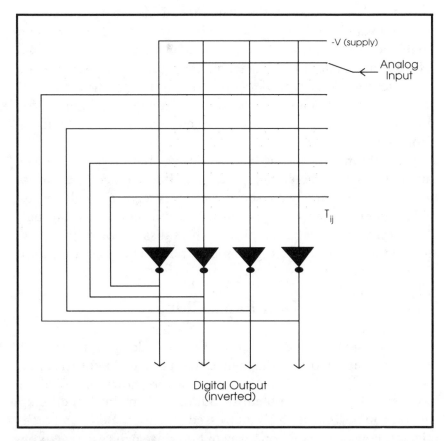

Hopfield's Analog-to-Digital Converter. Researcher John Hopfield was one of the first to cast neural designs into silicon microchips. Here his analog-to-digital converter uses the principle of energy minimization to work. The neuronlike amplifiers of Hopfield's first chip were connected with a square matrix of wires with resistive links at their intersections.

minimum according to a certain mathematical function. By varying the function, a researcher can cause the neural nets to cognize the solutions to computational problems. Hopfield's theory, unlike most theories of neural behavior, is simple enough to be constructed as real cognizer circuitry.

Accordingly, Hopfield teamed up with microchip experts at AT&T to realize his dream—microchips that emulate the brain. He is working with AT&T researcher David Tank to design circuits that are guided by the dynamics of his energy functions. The first standard problem tackled by Hopfield and Tank was an analog-to-digital signal converter—a circuit that turns real-world signals into a form readable by digital computers. While this circuit may seem trivial compared to state-of-the-art digital designs, it nevertheless demonstrates that a general method for emulating neurons can yield solutions to a variety of standard problems.

The only inherent limit for this design method is the power dissipation cost exacted by the resistive interconnections. Resistors create heat, and because these circuits require a high degree of interconnection—every amplifier must be connected through a resistor to every other amplifier—heat dissipation in the interconnect grid is the limiting factor on this sort of cognizer chip.

Bell Lab's Chips

Most of the components in Hopfield's simple design already exist in other integrated circuits, hence the methods of constructing them are well established. Accurate resistors, however, are often not needed and the problem of building them into microchip silicon had never been fully addressed. A team of Bell Lab's technicians, however, found one way of building such resistive interconnects with advanced semiconductor research apparatus. That newly developed method has allowed Bell Lab's researchers to build a 512-neuron chip with over 256,000 connections.

The 512 amplifiers are arranged in blocks of 128 around the edges of the chip. Resistors are built vertically at the 256,000

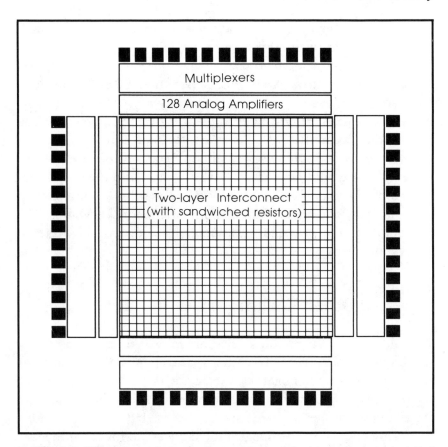

Bell Lab's Chip. One of the first cognizing microchips attempted at Bell Laboratories was fashioned after John Hopfield's theory. A dense matrix of tungsten wires in the center use a sandwiched layer of amorphous silicon to create resistive interconnections.

intersections of a central wire grid. A special, low-temperature ion beam process was used to place the resistors. The amplifiers and multiplexing circuitry are there only to minimize the number of external pins required by the chip.

Relatively coarse, two-micron (millionths of a meter) wide wires were used to build the AT&T chip. Bell Lab's researchers have already used electron beam techniques to build experimental interconnection matrices out of wire just 1000-angstrom (0.1 micron) wide. The ultimate limits of this technology could produce memory chips with 600 times the capacity of today's leading-edge digital memory chips.

Wires can be scaled down much more easily than digital devices. One thousand angstrom wires on 2,000-angstrom centers can be achieved today, a scale that allows a connection to be made in a 2,000 × 2,000-angstrom cell (0.2 microns square). The development of multilayered circuits has been slow because it is difficult to get a second layer of silicon to crystallize over a layer of devices. It would be feasible, however, to build the amplifiers in a Hopfield circuit on the first good crystalline layer and then lay down a second layer of amorphous silicon for the wiring. One by one, then, the practical problems of analog microchip technology are being overcome.

Other Techniques under Test

To build Hopfield-style chips, different microchip manufacturing techniques are being tried at other research labs. Researchers at the Jet Propulsion Laboratories (Pasadena, California) are working on a way to build into their chips resistances that change as the circuit operates. This resistance means that while Bell Lab's cognizing chips must be programmed once-and-for-all at the factory, JPL's chips will contain programmable connections that are determined by a learning process. The users of the JPL chips will be able to teach them to solve new problems.

Instead of being determined by manipulation of an energy-function equation, the resistances in JPL's chips are programmed by input from the external world. A resistance connection between two wires solidifies when voltages are applied across it. In the jargon of electronics, this type of device is a two-terminal, rather than three-terminal design. Most devices have three terminals: one for input, one for output, and one to control the flow of information. Neurons in Hopfield's model operate with only input and output. In accordance with Hebb's law, control is exerted by strengthening or weakening the connection between input and output through experience.

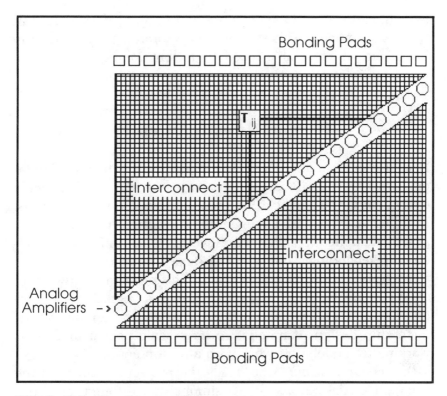

Mead's Chip. The first cognizing microchip built by Carver Mead improved upon Hopfield's original design by using programmable nodes (Tij) that could change, rather than depending upon preprogrammed resistive interconnections that could be set only once.

Carver Mead, a brilliant, innovative microchip designer, has long been an admirer of Hopfield. In 1984, Mead and his students fabricated an associative memory chip that included several clever design features. The chip consisted of 22 analog amplifiers arranged along the diagonal of a 22×22 cell array. The most innovative feature was the use of a dual-wire method to represent both excitatory and inhibitory connections, something not previously thought possible on a microchip.

When working, the Mead chip exhibited a feature of all Hopfield circuits—it continued to function even if devices within it failed. In fact, one chip had a component failure rate of over 50 percent and was still able to store two 22-bit vectors and recall them associatively. This sort of *failure softness* is also found in the brain, which is able to continue functioning even though neurons die daily.

Oregon Research Center

Neural models make unusual demands on electronic technology. The information capacity of a neural network is roughly equivalent to the density of interconnections between neurons. Building a device with enough interconnections to be useful for practical applications, however, overtakes not only current microchip technology, but also the most optimistic speculation about future microchip capabilities. This problem is now being addressed by the Oregon Graduate Center's Cognitive Architecture Project. The project, formed to study the application of microchip design techniques to large-scale neural models, is working to model a network with a billion connections.

Dan Hammerstrom, who heads the project, began with the Hopfield model because of its simplicity. He found, however, that the Hopfield model quickly becomes impractical because the length of wires increases in very large chips. To solve the problem, he examined experimental studies of how neurons in the brain handle long-distance communication. He found that while little is known about the fine details of these networks, one observation seemed to be an important clue—the probability of two neurons being interconnected falls off as the inverse of the distance between them.

This observation led Hammerstrom to use *locality of interconnection* as a basic working principle for the Cognitive Architecture Project's large-scale networks. Devices on CAP chips are always connected with their near neighbors, but as distance between devices increases, the number of connections drops off. In the future, this architecture may make a million-neuron system with a billion connections a reality.

One of the problems left open by Hammerstrom's attempt to build massively interconnected circuits is how they will be used to solve problems. Exactly how intelligent will such a network be? The number of neurons in the device makes it equivalent to the nervous system of a simple animal, but no one knows if this equation is a valid measure of intelligence. In fact, systems of this size with this degree of interconnectivity may prove to be unnecessary if the intricacies of the brain's network are unraveled. A more efficient use of resources might reduce the problems of building intelligent neural networks.

Grossberg's Microchips

Many principles that govern the action of actual neural networks are not being modeled by other cognizer designers. Stephen Grossberg, while mainly interested in understanding the brain, has come up with a list of the properties that, in his opinion, designers should seek to model.

One design principle Grossberg believes to be important in maintaining the stability of a neural net is the active regulation of neural activity. Hebb explained how the brain used coded synaptic weights, but Grossberg has shown that the passivity of Hebbian mechanics leads to instability. According to Grossberg's dynamic equations, only by adhering to the strict, active regulation of neural activity is stability guaranteed throughout the learning process, no matter how novel experiences become.

Chip designs patterned on Grossberg's equations will remain stable in the face of all possible experiences. With such chips, each long-term memory element (adaptive weight) is limited to oscillating only once during decision making. Absolute stability in this assured *ringing*—a pattern of mutually reinforcing oscillating waves that could overload a system—is damped out in a single cycle.

To make Grossberg's chips, neurons are modeled with charge packets transferred by using two kinds of semi-conductor devices now common in electronic components. Charge-coupled devices (CCDs) are strings of switches that transfer charges down a line like a bucket brigade. These devices are combined with the *floating gate* cell, another kind of cell that can store a charge the way a battery does. The two together imitate the action of the synapse in real neural networks. The CCDs transfer charge across the synapse, taking the role of chemical neurotransmitters, while the amount of charge transferred is set with the floating gate cell. The result is a connection whose conductance of electric charge can be precisely controlled. This combination will produce programmable devices with standard semiconductor technology.

TRW, Too

TRW is another major electronics concern doing pioneering work with cognizers. At TRW's San Diego Artificial Intelligence Research Center, Robert Hecht-Nielsen built a digital computer that solves Grossberg's equations. By following Grossberg's design principles, Hecht-Nielsen emulated neural networks at high speed. This unit was offered in 1986 as the first commercial neural network, albeit only for researchers interested in studying these models in greater detail.

This ability of digital computers to solve dynamic equations at high speed brings the TRW machine close in performance to an electrical network that Grossberg described on paper. This network can be programmed to process visual and auditory signals into meaningful units. For instance, information from a video camera is a varying signal that could represent anything. The TRW machine can take this signal and find either geometric structures or three-dimensional scenes within it.

Summary

Research in ways to capture neural networks in silicon has made remarkable progress in the last few years, and with major research efforts being made in the United States, Europe, and Japan, even more progress will be forthcoming. Armed with a deeper understanding of the workings of the brain, researchers will have the practical experience that enables them to construct devices capable of embodying this knowledge, making cognizers a practical possibility. With the many excellent microchip designers who are pursuing neural networks, the building blocks for cognizers will soon be widely available.

7

Fledgling Cognizers

Need a Computer or a Cognizer?

Commercial cognizer chips may never be necessary if die-hard digital designers have their way. Proponents claim that current digital systems can mimic many of the properties of neurons in software. The result may be artificial intelligence that is fundamentally different from the expert systems currently in vogue. Whether built in hardware or software, they are the beginning of a new kind of machine intelligence that transcends the label artificial.

Pioneers in cognizer architecture find themselves in a curious situation. Rather than charting new territories with shiny new circuits, they are resurrecting precomputer technologies. Building cognizer circuitry means backtracking to where the perceptron and digital computer parted ways in the 1960s. The cognizer industry is now showing many of the growing pains seen in the early computer industry. Patching together the bulky, clumsy circuitry needed to test a possible neural architecture can be a self-defeating task. Therefore, many researchers have turned to simulating the actions of neurons with digital circuitry and software.

Crawling before Walking

Digital computers are capable of imitating the behavior of analog neural networks although they do so much more slowly than custom-designed, analog chips. Software emulation of many thousands of neurons has been achieved on supercomputers, and useful work has also been done by simulations with as few as six neurons.

Concurrent computers—computers composed of many microprocessors running simultaneously—also work well emulating cognizers, even though they were designed to solve computationally difficult engineering problems. The simultaneous operation of many small processors matches the parallel operation of neurons in the brain better than the serial operation of a single processor system.

One of these large parallel computers was used at the University of Rochester to perform the largest neural simulation every tried. The computer called the *Butterfly* was developed by the Bolt, Bareneck, and Newman company with funding from the government's Defense Advanced Research Projects Agency (DARPA). The Butterfly is not quite a supercomputer but is one of a class of computers that has appeared in the past few years called budget supercomputers. These new machines take advantage of the latest integrated-circuit technology to provide exceptionally high computational capabilities at a cost far below that of supercomputers.

The University of Rochester simulation experiment gives some idea of how close supercomputers come to imitating the brain. The program can simulate a maximum of one one-hundred-thousandth of the neurons in the brain and one ten-billionth of the connections. Those kinds of numbers make it appear that computers can accomplish almost nothing when trying to imitate directly the operation of the brain. What is surprising, though, is how effective even such small models can be in performing useful cognitive operations.

Talking Cognizers

One project where simulations of neural nets are proving useful is speech synthesis. Terrence Sejnowski at Johns Hopkins University has created a neural-based simulation system that can read text and synthesize speech. By programming a minicomputer to simulate a hypothetical analog *learning circuit,* he demonstrated the feasibility of machines that can speak.

By using Rumelhart's back-propagation of errors approach, Sejnowski created a simulated circuit that processes written text to produce a spoken output. Sejnowski teaches his system to read text, not by programming, but by allowing it to learn for itself. The software simulator learns English the same way humans do, by *listening* to correct examples of English pronunciation (stored in files in the computer) while *watching* the words

Terrence Sejnowski. The neural simulator built by Terrence Sejnowski learned to speak English by observing words while "listening" to a child reading. It achieved in 16 hours of learning what it took 20 man-years of programming to accomplish.

(in text files) and trying to pronounce them. The result of Sejnowski's learning program is eerie. The system starts with a random set of values in its learning circuits and results in an output from the speech synthesizer that is a continuous, voiced wail with no intelligible characteristics. But after some training sessions, the adjusted system begins to understand that letters are grouped into units people call words. Although the system continues to mispronounce, its babble suddenly starts to sound more human, almost babylike, because the division of a sentence into words produces the familiar rhythm of continuous speech. Then gradually, after repeated learning sessions, meaningful sounds (for a trained listener) begin to emerge.

The program reads seven characters at a time, attempting to match a sound to the letter in the center of the sequence of seven. The reason for using a sequence of characters to calculate the sound of a single character is that context affects the way a character is pronounced. Depending on the letters that surround it, the same letter must be matched with different sounds, a process which is what makes language so difficult for computers—there is no simple set of rules that covers all situations without exception.

By giving it correct examples to ponder, Sejnowski taught his programmed neural model (called NETalk) to match sounds with the letters. After a mere 16 hours of this training, the computer could read the 100-word example text with 98 percent accuracy—about a third-grade reading level in less than one day! Even more remarkable, the system knew how to read other, similar texts presented to it with almost the same accuracy. Sejnowski used a child's essay as the training passage because he wanted a realistic example of English, rather than something that was rule perfect.

The significant aspect of Sejnowski's machine is that it does not start with a preprogrammed set of pronunciation rules. A collaborator of Sejnowski's, however, Charles Rosenberg, developed a mathematical system for analyzing how a back-propagation network represents concepts. This analysis system is able to look at the weight that results from a training session and produce a map of the cognitive model it represents. Rosenberg's analysis of

NETalk showed that the network does form an articulated model of vowels, even though it was not supplied with any model at all. This kind of analysis supports the claim that neural networks can come up with knowledge models on their own.

Sejnowski's talking neural simulator was inspired by a Digital Equipment Corporation research project called DECtalk. DECtalk can read English characters and produce the correct pronunciations with about 95 percent accuracy. DECtalk, however, is based on rules of English pronunciation derived by a team of linguists and, as might be expected, contains a large dictionary of exceptions. The system first checks the exception list and then proceeds to apply its linguistic rules. It took 20 years to perfect DECtalk. Sejnowski claims he was able to put together his system over a summer vacation and, in about 16 hours, teach it to read nearly as well as DECtalk.

How It Works

Sejnowski's computer system calculates the response of a mere 300 neurons with 18,000 electronically weighted connections. Not only is this a small number of neurons, but the neural model itself is very crude compared to the large variety of behaviors observed with real neurons. The 300-neuron network matches sequences of 0s and 1s representing letters with sequences of 0s and 1s representing an alphabet of sounds that people use when speaking. These units of speech are called *phonemes* by linguists: As is the case with any other alphabet, there is only a small number of them.

The problem of getting an artificial neural network to read is, therefore: Some procedure must be found to alter the sequence of 0s and 1s representing a letter into a sequence representing the sound of that letter. If each letter in English corresponded with a unique sound, no matter where that letter appeared in a word, the problem would be very easy to solve. Unfortunately the context in which a letter appears determines the correct sound as much as the letter itself.

Once the correct sequence of phonemes has been identified, these units of speech can be fed to a sound synthesizer designed to produce a facsimile of human speech. In his reading system, Sejnowski used a synthesizer built by the DECtalk team.

Sejnowski's system starts with a random setting for its synaptic weights, then modifies these weights to change the behavior of the network. Researchers now know that the brain uses this same method to remember and learn new things, but exactly how the brain accomplishes this process is a subject of intense debate. Sejnowski's system demonstrated that Rummelhart's back-propagation of errors method can lead to effective learning in a viable cognizing system.

Beyond Perceptrons

Many neural simulations have not improved since McCulloch and Pitts' work in the early 1940s. Almost all current attempts at building such simulations use the simplified threshold model. Grossberg's theoretical models have shown how more complicated aspects of neural behavior can be used to perform needed functions in cognitive processing, but these more realistic models also require more specialized hardware.

The next step in developing this hardware is to build digital circuits dedicated to emulating neural behavior. Though the circuits would still suffer from the essential mismatch between the digital gate and the neuron, they would work more quickly than conventional digital circuits. Both University researchers and electronics companies are currently hard at work on circuits and systems that can emulate nerve networks more accurately. The first such system to appear on the market was TRW's Artificial Neural System (ANS) processor, produced by Robert Hecht-Nielsen. Hecht-Nielsen built ANS Mark III to provide emulating performance equivalent to 10 minicomputers running neural simulation software.

The Mark III is housed in a three-cubic-foot enclosure that attaches directly to a conventional VAX minicomputer. It is used with a color graphics display and a set of software utilities—the Artificial Neural System Environment—for setting up and reviewing the results of neural simulations. The Mark III can simulate up to 8,100 neurons and either 417,700 interconnections with variable weights or 1.2 million interconnections with fixed weights.

TRW's program to develop artificial neural systems is one of the most ambitious in the world. This program is heavily defense-oriented, since it began with a contract from the Defense Advanced Research Projects Agency (DARPA). The Mark III, already proven in speech recognition applications, was followed by the Mark IV, a more advanced model designed to process data as it arrives—that is in *real-time*.

Hecht-Nielsen Neurocomputer

Robert Hecht-Nielsen, the mastermind behind TRW's artificial neural system, started a small, innovative company dedicated to translating neural-network theory into simulating electronic circuitry. Hecht-Nielsen Neurocomputer Corporation started out small by offering a modified IBM personal computer that comes with a month-long course in neural-network theory. Companies wanting to develop this kind of technology can send one of their experts to the course along with some unsolved problem. Solutions to the problem are developed as part of the training.

Hecht-Nielsen strongly believes in this sort of *clinical* experience for developing the new technology because so few engineers understand the nervous system. Neural behavior is much more complex than computer behavior and much more difficult to predict from theory. As in medical training, experience with what can go wrong with *live* systems is necessary to develop a full range of expertise in neural-network technology.

Hecht-Nielsen's company is also pioneering a new computer language, *Axon*, that is designed for programming digital computers to imitate neural networks. Hecht-Nielsen chose the digital simulation route because it was the fastest way to build a

Robert Hecht-Nielsen. A long time Grossberg admirer, Robert Hecht-Nielsen made the first commercial neural net at TRW Inc. and subsequently started one of the first companies dedicated to building neurocomputers—simulated cognizers embedded into a host computer.

company. He expects to branch out eventually into other technologies such as analog electronic circuits or light-based optical methods. He feels that by working with clients and their real world problems, the right development path will unfold.

Anderson's Cognizer

In the threshold model of neural behavior, the neuron fires only if the weighted sum of its inputs rises above a predefined threshold value. In Geoffrey Hinton's and Terrence Sejnowski's Boltzmann Machine, the weighted sum is operated on by a probability function to determine firing frequency. In Grossberg's models, this sum is operated on by a sigmoid function that can be tuned to filter out signals below some predetermined level. All of these techniques are difficult to model on a digital computer because they use complex mathematics to determine their outputs.

James Anderson of Brown University eliminated many of these mathematical complications to construct a simple auto-associative memory that is more compatible with digital computers. In Anderson's model memory, each neuron takes as its output the weighted sum of its inputs. This system acts much as a conventional AI expert system. In fact, Anderson started with the same application area that spawned expert systems: a medical database. Anderson's associative memory is very effective at matching symptoms with a prescribed drug and alerting the physician to unwanted side effects of the prescription.

The lack of a neural-transfer function allows Anderson's system to respond to queries that it has never seen before and which have nothing to do with the original body of knowledge programmed into the database. Anderson contends that the information volunteered by his system often resembles a very shrewd guess. These responses would be eliminated with a more rigid neural simulation, but Anderson has decided they should be viewed as an advantage. People should expect complex neural systems to produce unexpected results as part of the richer set of behavior responses.

Anderson's systems, though, are not designed to further an understanding of how neural networks operate. His main concern is using the insights from neural activity to build better expert systems.

Current optical technology presents two drawbacks to computer designers: The components are large and cumbersome (like electronic components of the 1950s), and the methods by which the hardware operates do not lend themselves to current architectures. But, Ravindra Athale, a researcher at BDM Corporation, has begun to overcome these two drawbacks. Athale found that by adjusting theory to match available devices he could achieve results with a few inexpensive, off-the-shelf, light-emitting diodes (LEDs) and photodetectors.

By altering algorithms that were inspired by neural studies, Athale corrected the mismatch between theory and hardware. He found a way of compensating for the lower interconnection densities of optical systems by doing more processing with the LEDs and photodetectors. His associative memory also has new capabilities: It can be programmed with advance knowledge that influences its memory operation. This ability means that it can be predisposed to absorb certain types of information and ignore everything else.

Demetri Psaltis, an optical researcher at California Institute of Technology, believes the associative-memory theory developed by scientists like Athale, Grossberg, and Hopfield can be applied to an existing technology—optical disks. In recent years, optical disks have been developed in recent years that far exceed magnetic and semiconductor-based memory systems in storage capacity. Internally, optical disks use laser technology to store and retrieve information on a special optical medium. Externally, this optically encoded information is converted to electronic form for digital computer manipulation.

Psaltis is working on a design for a massively parallel read-head for optical disks, one that can read up to a million bits simultaneously where current read-heads pick up only one bit at a time. The parallel read-head could handle gigabytes of information. Psaltis believes that compact laser systems

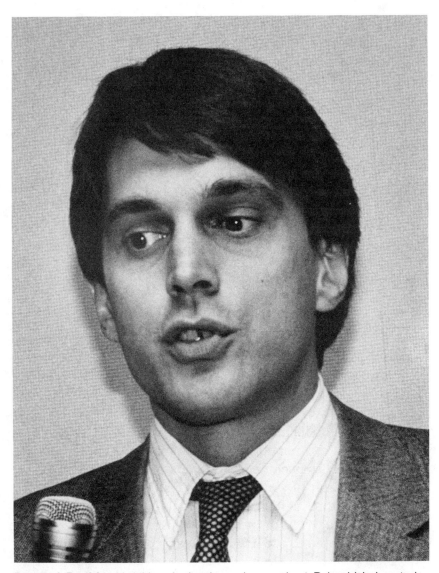

Demetri Psaltis. Van Heerden's pioneering work at Polaroid Laboratories has been continued by Demetri Psaltis and his co-workers at the University of California. However, Psaltis has abandoned traditional digital technologies in favor of novel optical implementations.

developed for optical disk products could be used to implement this design.

This parallel read-head could be used with another innovation—read-write disks. Current optical disks are read-only devices—data can be taken from the disk, but new information cannot be stored on it. However, new media that allow magnetic fields to change the optical properties of a material will soon make possible large-scale read-and-write memories. Psaltis suggests that his parallel read-head could feed data to an electronic computer that could then return processed data to the disk. This system would essentially be a new kind of database.

The aspect of this approach that interests us here is that pre-processing can be done with special optical components in the read-head. Rather than simply piping massive amounts of data to the computer, this optical read-head retrieves data by association. A feedback loop to the disk would turn this large, optical storage unit into a massive associative memory that could adapt to new information as it is processed. An adaptive-associative memory like this one would allow the computer to receive relevant information immediately. Also, data organization would reflect the history of the whole system, producing a more integrated relationship between processor and memory.

The key to producing this kind of intelligent, parallel optical read-head lies in a network of simple analog computational elements. Psaltis has become a proponent of analog processor networks as a result of some hard lessons in trying to implement digital algorithms with optical technology. He eventually became discouraged with attempts to use digital techniques in optics and turned to the analog-network approach.

Real Optical Systems

An optical computer designed at the Naval Research Laboratory is sorting out the information coming from many different radar units. In theory, it takes only two different readings to fix the location of a target. But in a modern battle, a multitude of sensors are tracking a multitude of targets, and suddenly the problem of locating each one becomes enormously difficult to compute.

Harold Szu, an optical expert at the Naval Lab, found a unique type of Boltzmann machine that is ideal for optical technology. Not only is this new version well-matched to optical electronics, it is also often faster than Hinton's and Sejnowski's original design.

This machine is based on a type of probability calculation first discovered by the nineteenth-century mathematician Augustin-Louis Cauchy. Although few real-world uses for Cauchy's probability theory have been found, the calculations it describes can be done very quickly. Szu constructed a virtual network of analog processors connected in a way similar to neurons in the brain. The input to the network are the signals from a set of radar sensors, and the outputs are the location of the targets.

Szu's network is set up so that the best interpretation of the data is represented by its lowest energy state. The algorithm for

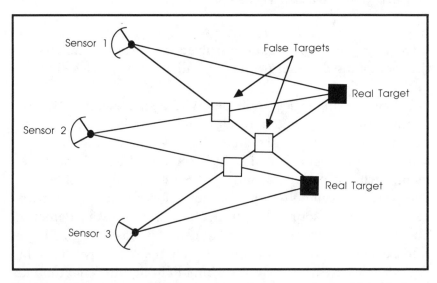

Ghosts. Many sensors viewing many targets can create ghost images (gray shading). These false target locations can greatly complicate a computer's attempt to find the real targets, but Harold Szu's optical version of the Cauchy machine sorts them out easily.

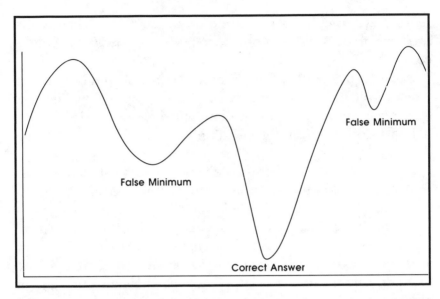

False Minimum. Energy minimization circuitry is tuned to relax into its lowest energy state to arrive at correct answers. But a careless design can cause the circuit to temporarily get caught up in false minimums. Total relaxation of the circuit yields the correct answer.

discovering the lowest state is solved by an optical processor that computes the energy states of all network nodes simultaneously.

The processing is accomplished with a stacked array of light sources that are rotated randomly to simulate the random fluctuations in a physical system (e.g., a fluid). Facing this light-source array is an array of light detectors. With this arrangement, each source can partially contribute to the output of each detector. To accomplish this process electronically would require that every source be physically wired to every detector. The network is programmed to perform its tasks by placing a transparency in front of the detectors that selectively filters the light that reaches them. By absorbing light in different amounts at each connection, the transparency can produce a set of weights that encode the target resolution problem.

Even in the absence of advanced analog microchips, much

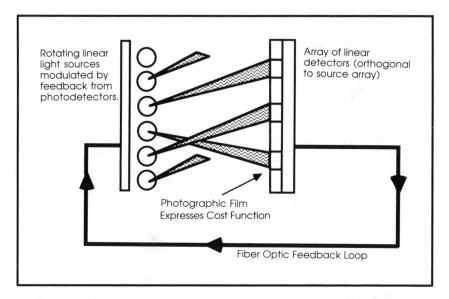

Optical Cauchy. The Naval Research Lab has used simple optical components to imitate neurons with light, rather than electricity. Gray areas on a
photographic film were formed into the weighted interconnections among an
array of simulated neurons.

work is being done in the development of cognizers. Neural nets,
for instance, can be simulated through existing digital and optical technologies. In spite of their limits, use of these medias has
allowed an understanding of cognizer circuitry to grow, even
while awaiting the perfection of analog microchips.

8

Cognizers of the Mind

If Their Bodies Are Perfected, Will They Have Minds?

The initial reaction to cognizers is often one of fear—the perennial fear of creating an intelligence that could make obsolete man's intelligence. Cognizers may be able to learn, but even if they can imitate all sorts of human abilities, will they ever be said to have minds?

The basic confusion associated with asking such questions about machines is that there is no agreement about what it is to have minds. The private realm of mind-stuff has resisted detailed scientific exploration. In the course of answering the question "do cognizers have minds?", perhaps scientists will clarify what it is for people to have minds.

But the real promise of the coming cognizer revolution remains obscure. It will surely be as magnificent and unimaginable as the modern computer was to the inventor of the punched computer card in the eighteenth century (whose application was a programmable fabric weaver).

Shortly after inventing the stored program computer, John von Neumann began speculating on the status of automatic machines. His conclusion was that until they can be constructed in such a way that they can reproduce, they will remain mere *soul-less automata*. But no one has yet seriously attempted building self-reproducing automata.

Before the turn of the century, though, a complete mapping is likely to have been made correlating a multitude of thinking- , emotional- , and memory-states with unique physiological conditions. With such a map, future cognizer designers will merely have to follow the directions in a *Cognizer Cookbook* to brew up whatever intelligent functionality they desire. Prewired cognizer microchips, now being built in prototype form by AT&T and others, will offer self-contained, functional modules of various cognitive types.

The cognizer revolution will be a slow growing one, with special-purpose subsystems at first merely augmenting traditional electronic technologies. When autonomous cognizers are fully functioning, however, what will their status be? Cognizers are built to contain their *I* in short-term memory—the common repository for perceptions just cognized and memories recognized from the past. Their mind, if they can be said to have one, will be an immaterial analog of the activity that is going on in that short-term memory.

The same is true for humans. What people call the mind's ideas are really immaterial analogs to the actual physical activity in the brain. *Immaterial* here does not mean *parapsychological*, but merely refers to the fact that an idea does not take up any physical space. There are a number of familiar things that are immaterial in this sense—anger, beauty, value, or the government. There are also physical objects usually associated with these immaterial analogs—harsh words, objects of art, or a collection of buildings. Since these objects cannot be precisely identified with the immaterial realities associated with them, however, the question then becomes, will cognizers also share in this whole world of immaterial concepts and ideas? Or will they still be mindless artificial intelligences that merely mimic life?

Can Machines Ever Have Minds?

Perhaps the most controversial issue that cognizer research addresses is the age-old problem of the mind and body. Both the body of a human and the mechanism of a cognizer can be said to have thoughts, if *thought* is defined as the act of cognition (the cognition of sensations into perceptions or the recognition of sensations from memory). But can cognizers be said to have minds?

This question comes down to the relationship between the mind and the body. Is the mind identical with the body, or is it a separate entity? It is easy to accept that the word *mind* can have an immaterial meaning, but there are not necessarily any immaterial substances that correlate to the concept of mind. After all, there is no single immaterial substance that corresponds to the government.

If the mind and body are the same, however, then what do people mean by statements about thoughts, feelings, judgments, expectations, or intentions? Do these statements simply refer to minute physical events in the brain? How can hopes, fears, moods, humor, and motives really be physical events in the body?

On the other hand, if the stuff of mind is not of the body, then how can an immaterial thing like a decision have any effect on the physical world? How can ideas, which are without weight or size, influence the course of events in the brain? If immaterial thoughts can move cells in the brain, then why are they confined to a single skull? What keeps an immaterial thing "in there"?

Philosophers have been proposing answers to these questions for millennia. It appears that science, through neural and cognizer research, may be able to contribute to an answer. Before examining the extent to which this research addresses these questions, it will be useful to examine the various historical philosophical positions.

History of Ideas

Plato was the first western philosopher to make a sharp distinction between the mind and the body. He held that the mind had existed before birth and would endure after its residence in the body was over. Many medieval philosophers, while denying pre-existence, accepted and emphasized the immaterial separateness of mind, especially its immortality. St. Augustine and Thomas Aquinas built philosophies that were in many ways polar opposites, yet were both based on the distinction between the material and spiritual realms.

In the seventeenth century, René Descartes also originated a systematic doctrine of mind/body relations. Descartes taught that both the mind and the body were substances, but with very different basic natures. Body is extended in space and unthinking, while mind is thinking but not extended in space. By isolating extension in space as the deciding factor between mind and matter, Descartes secularized the concept of mind.

Though Descartes' concept of mind was not tied to religion, it was still far from being a scientific theory. Mental substance, called *pure ego* by Descartes, was a nonextended stuff that can nevertheless undergo changes. Furthermore, to maintain its existence, this pure thinking substance must always be thinking.

Descartes held that animals lacked this thinking substance entirely, though he recognized that they were capable of feelings. But man, for Descartes, was composed of both mind and matter so inextricably intertwined that the one can cause the other to do things. For Descartes, mental substance obviously moved physical substance. How else could you continue reading this page? One's immaterial decision to read on causes one's material eyes to keep moving.

Interactionists

Descartes' concept of the relationship between mind and body is referred to as *interactionist* because it allows interaction between mind and body. Not only does the physical cause the mental (tooth decay causes toothache), but the mental causes the physical as well (toothache causes a phone call to dentist). Strictly speaking, to be an interactionist, one does not have to accept Descartes' notion of a mental substance. Immanuel Kant, for instance, rejected this concept, arguing that Descartes mistakenly granted metaphysical status to the merely logical requirement for a subject to whom to ascribe judgments. There must be an *I* to be the subject, but that requirement does not mean the *I* is in some sort of invisible world. In spite of rejecting Descartes' notion of a mental substance, Kant went on to develop an interactionist philosophy.

Still, there are several empirical objections to the interactionist doctrine that make it highly suspect. First, it appears to violate the principle of the conservation of matter and energy, which maintains that physical effects in one part of the world must use energy from another part of the world. How can mental events affect the world, if they are outside of space? An interactionist might answer this criticism by denying that the conservation principle holds between two realms, yet if the realms are held to be so dissimilar that they transcend matter and energy conservation, then how can a causal connection hold between mental states and brain states? If they are so utterly different, how can they interact?

Gottfried Leibniz, contemporary of Newton and co-inventor of mathematical calculus, offered a possible answer to these questions. He held that the two realms—physical and mental—acted in parallel, that every mental event correlates with some other physical event, but not causally. Whenever one occurs, then the other inevitably occurs, but this constant conjunction is not a causal connection. Examples of this kind of conjunction appear in the physical world. For instance, there is a correlation every summer between the number of ice cream cones sold and the number of children drowned. Both increase simultaneously, but it is recognized that one does not cause the other. Leibniz held that a similar conjunction occurred in the immaterial realm of minds, but with more complex rules ʰthan simple simultaneity. For Leibniz, minds and bodies were replaced with an infinity of spirits, each going inexorably through its own unfolding and all related to another, not by causation, but by being mirror images of one another.

Critics of this parallelism point out that people accept many other physical relations as causal with no more evidence than can be produced for mental events. As mental functioning is increasingly correlated with identifiable mechanisms in the brain, however, there is bound to be mounting evidence for some sort of parallelism. Since mental substance will always remain immaterial, there may never be a way to determine empirically whether thoughts influence brain mechanisms or whether the two are merely parallel. There appears to be no conceivable way to choose between the two views.

Epiphenomenalism

Epiphenomenalism is a philosophical approach that answers the objections to both interactionism and parallelism. It deals with the difficulty in explaining how mental events can cause physical events by denying that they do. Causality goes only from the physical to the mental and not the other way around; thus, mental events are only symptoms of the underlying physical events that are the real causes.

Epiphenomenalists give a full account of human behavior in terms of bodily states, with special attention to brain states. The apparent ability of mental events to cause physical ones is considered an illusion. Though it may seem that mental wishes and desires are the causes of physical actions, in fact, they are mere by-products of physical processes. When you touch a hot stove, physical events in the brain cause you to pull your hand away. The hot feeling is not the cause of the removal of your hand, but merely an accompanying effect. An automata would also remove its appendage, but would not have a mental feeling of pain.

Critics point out that when all is said and done, there is still a nagging feeling that thoughts *do* cause physical events. Epiphenomenalists hope that someday soon neurophysiology may give a complete account of behavior without the need to resort to mental events. Nevertheless, epiphenomenalists contend, it will continue to be correct in a sense to say, "The pain caused me to remove my hand from the hot stove," just as it is still correct to say "The sun rose this morning." Describing our actions as if they were caused by thoughts and emotions will still be an accurate description of what we experience, even though those experiences do not strictly conform to reality.

Evidence

How one views the mental realm of feelings, thought, and remembrances depends upon whether or not you believe the mind can cause events in the external world. Epiphenomenalists hold that the body affects the mind and not vice versa. The interactionist objects that immaterial thoughts like a decision to act followed by action are proof for mental causes of physical effects, and the parallelist says both are simultaneous, and that is all that can be said.

Several contemporary issues could, if resolved, provide guidance for choosing among the three positions. Some parapsychological studies hold that the mental events of one person can directly affect the thought of another without a physical connection. If this phenomenon could be proven, it could sway the argument in favor of interactionism, since parallelism and epiphenomenalism both isolate the mental side too effectively for any sort of mind-to-mind communication. Unfortunately, any

conceivable demonstration of such a parapsychological phenomenon will probably not convince the skeptic. Mind-to-mind
communication presupposes the absence of physical causes, and
a skeptic will merely assume that the phenomena are caused by
an as yet undetected physical mechanism.

The advent of cognizers raises some interesting questions in
connection with this topic. There is no mental side designed into
cognizers, which means that if they are fully developed, they will
argue against extreme interactionists who require mental substance. A weak interactionist could conceivably maintain that
cognizers can have mental events by virtue of an "anything is
possible" argument. After all, we really know very little about
the mental domain. But strong interactionists hold that substan-
tial mental phenomena are necessary for cognition. A strong
interactionist could also hold that a mind could spontaneously
arise in a cognizer, but such a spontaneous development would
also support epiphenomenalism. Epiphenomenalism and parallelism can both tolerate cognizers that mimic a person, but
strong interactionism requires that this special stuff called *mind*
be present.

Rest of the World

Epiphenomenalism, interactionism, and parallelism represent
only half the spectrum of mind/body theories. These three are
all dualisms because they maintain that there are two worlds—
the mental and the physical. For epiphenomenalism, while the
mental is a mere effect of the physical world, it is still recogniz-
ably distinct.

There is another possible alternative to all three of these dualisms: monism. Believers in monism maintain that both the physical and mental realms are just two sides of the same coin. Just
how that coin metaphor is interpreted determines the brands of
monism.

Materialism, for instance, holds that statements about mental
events are at best synonymous with reports of physical events

and at worst meaningless. Such psychological behaviorism or *physicalism*, as philosophers call it, has been supported by renowned thinkers from Ivan Pavlov to Vienna-circle philosopher Rudolf Carnap. All claimed that every statement about thoughts, feelings, and remembrances could be plausibly translated into physical terms. Materialism is the predominant view of many hardnosed scientists who are determined that nothing will be considered real that cannot be quantified.

A less strict monism holds that, though statements about mental and physical expressions differ in significance or connotation, they actually denote one and the same physical phenomena. Just as the phrases *the evening star* and *the morning star* have different connotations even though both refer to the planet Venus, statements about brain states and ideas mean different things while referring to the same objects. This empirical identity—as opposed to logical identity—maintains that each particular mental event has an analog in a particular brain state. Thus mental and neural events are one and the same thing—physical.

Critics against identity theory point out that it makes sense to ask where a neural event occurs in the body, but it makes no sense to ask where in the body the thought occurred. A pain in the foot is not in the brain but in the foot. How can the mental and physical events be the same if they do not occur in same place? Of course, the materialist will reply that the nervous system exists throughout the body and therefore in the foot as well, but this reply misses the point. There is no physical event in the body that you can point to and say, "There, that is his pain." The pain that one feels is not available for public scrutiny.

Another objection to identity theory is that it cannot account for the privileged position of a subject to know his or her own thoughts and feelings. Each person lives within a private world of thoughts, feelings, and remembrances. If these thoughts and emotions were all just ordinary physical events, then why is the subject in such a privileged position to report them without observation or inference? Thought, feelings, and remembrances pop into and out of the mind uninvited. If they are simply physical, then why do they never boil over into other brains nearby?

Subjective Idealism

Descartes found one thing he could not doubt: the existence of his own mind. He could deny that animals had thought, he could deny that the world existed, but he couldn't deny that he existed because denial assumed the existence of a denier. From this point, Descartes eventually demonstrated the real existence of the world, other minds, and God. But Bishop George Berkeley took the method of doubting everything that can be doubted to its logical extreme, maintaining that only the *I* and its perceptions are truly real.

Berkeley took the opposite tack from the materialist and identity theorists by arguing that all physical statements are really about mental phenomena. Berkeley's argument was that one could wake up at any moment and find that he or she was dreaming. Therefore, the only thing that is totally trustworthy are perceptions themselves with no presuppositions about what they are based on—material stuff or dream stuff was all the same to Berkeley.

Berkeley recognized that the most trustworthy thing that an *I* can have is a perception. A drunk may deny that the pink elephants he sees really exist, but he cannot deny that he sees them. Cognizer theory similarly recognizes experience as a pattern of activity partly caused by sensation and partly caused by remembrances. The two sorts of perception mix at the *I*, the only thing anyone can really trust.

For Berkeley, the mind and its thoughts, feelings, and remembrances were the only things of which people could be sure. Berkeley expanded this insight into a full-blown philosophy which maintained that the perceptions of minds are the only things that really exist. Physical objects, for Berkeley, existed only in the mind as classes of perceptions. Statements about the physical world are meaningful only when they are taken as statements about the perceptions of perceivers. All objects therefore exist only in the mind.

Berkeley's viewpoint represents the last vestige of safety for the thoroughgoing skeptic. Perceptions of the world, taken at face value and not as indicators of enduring objects, provide a rockbottom basis for belief. Yet this position is not a satisfying one for several reasons. Under this analysis, the perceptions of the insane are just as valid as those of normal people. Furthermore, Berkeley's position cannot explain the consensus that separate perceivers have when observing the same phenomena. Though Berkeley's view might provide a solid basis for belief, it is not a theory that helps developing scientists very much.

Spinoza answered the criticism of parallelism by claiming that causality is a precise analog of logical deduction, but while he agreed that the physical world was not real, he did not doom it to illusion as Berkeley did. For Spinoza, the mental and physical were simply different aspects of something that was neither mental nor physical. Spinoza believed that the physical and the mental could yield full descriptions of man, but under different categories. Panpsychists, like Spinoza, held further that all physical entities have a corresponding mental aspect—even rocks.

The main problem with panpsychism lies in the conception of an underlying unity. If the mental cannot be reduced to the physical (materialism), and the physical cannot be reduced to the mental (idealism), then how will some unseen third thing, of which the mental and physical are two aspects, help very much? Why is there a need for aspects anyway? Occam's razor—a philosophical principle that says take the simplest explanation— dictates that if mental and physical reality are merely two viewpoints on some third thing, and that third thing is indescribable, then it is unnecessary. This unseen reality is simply a metaphor that further obscures an already difficult subject. How is one even supposed to understand what *viewpoint* or *aspect* means if it is not in mental or physical terms?

David Hume tried to overcome the problem of monism by contending that both mental and physical entities are composed of the same bundles of perceptions. The individual was thus simply a repository for these perceptions, which succeed each other ceaselessly. According to Hume, people organize individual perceptions into naturally occurring bundles by their resemblance, endurance through time, and apparent causal connections. Memory, Hume suggested, was the key condition to identifying objects, uncovering causal relations, and maintaining one's individuality.

This view has been quite popular with others through the years. William James called these bundles of perceptions the *neutral stuff of pure experience*. Ernst Mach called them the *neutral entities of sensation*, while Bertrand Russell called them *sensibilia* and argued that mind and matter were both merely logical constructions out of sensibilia. Some years later, the logical positivist A. J. Ayer came up with a view that updated the bundle of perception approach by advocating that mental and physical statements could both be translated into statements about sensation.

All these views, grouped together as neutral monism, are subject to several criticisms. For one, events are said to belong to a person if they are capable of being remembered by that person. Thus, resemblance theories of reality depend upon events that occur in a single mind. But if mental events are separate and autonomous, then by what principle could they be connected to form a mind? Either the unity of the mind is simply another perception, or it violates the monism. If the mind is just another perception, however, how can it form the basis for unifying perceptions?

Stream-of-Consciousness Theory

William James came up with a solution to all these problems with the concept of a *stream of consciousness*. James' theory is an intermediary between mental substances and bundles of perceptions. This theory emphasizes the continuity of experience by defining a person as an unbroken stream-of-consciousness.

Unfortunately, James' view is more a stopgap measure to evade criticism than a real attempt to explain things. For instance, what about sleep and comas? How can individuals endure such gaps of unconsciousness? Relating the stream of consciousness to a particular body would guarantee continuity, even in unconsciousness, but would not be a monism. It also rules out existence after death, unless disembodied mental events can exist without a mind to think them!

Disembodied existence might sound like a doubtful concept, but it has been advocated by many well-respected men and women. In fact, many people deny materialism, identity theory, double-aspect theory, parallelism, and epiphenomenalism because they conflict with the idea of disembodied existence. Disembodied existence is compatible with idealism, neutral monism, and interactionism.

Against disembodied existence it can be argued that neural mechanisms appear to be necessary for consciousness to exist. All natural objects that appear to have consciousness also have nervous systems. Since all neural mechanisms cease functioning entirely after death, consciousness probably ceases, too. It could be argued that consciousness depends on the body only as long as a person is in it and is liberated after death, a position supported by reports of the near-dead. But such evidence can also be explained as aberrant perceptions in a faulty nervous system.

Contemporary philosophers dismiss most of the monistic theories because they cannot give an adequate account of individuality. P. F. Strawson, for one, contends that a person can be defined only as an individual made up of both states of consciousness and physical characteristics—a form of dualism.

Although many monistic theories attempt to define an individual by linking current mental events with the individual's memories, this definition really misses the point. Memory of earlier mental events must be in the mind that experienced the events. Thus, memory presupposes the concept of the enduring mind and cannot be used to explain it. This same argument can be used against the possibility that the neutral entitles of perception can congeal into distinct physical objects.

Origin of the *I*

Cognizer research has provided an answer to how memory can define an *I*. Franz Brentano provided the clue when he suggested that mental phenomena are *intentional*—that they contain an object in themselves. Thoughts about objects *intend* the object itself even if the object does not really exist. Brentano claimed that intentional phenomena could not be analyzed into purely physical terms, but cognizer research has shown how that very thing can in fact be done.

The reason ideas resemble the objects they denote is that the act of cognition transforms sensation into clear and distinct perceptions of objects and stores features of the objects in memory. Then, when thinking about that type of object, people recognize its features from their representation in memory. The remembrance resembles the original object because it is an echo of the original perception of it. Man's memory circuitry is set up to return a perception into short-term memory that resembles the original because it is composed of features extracted from that original perception and stored away in memory. The *I* is the place where remembrances are played back, using the identical circuitry that takes in perceptions from the outside world. Together the perceptions from outside and remembrances from inside resonate in the common repository of short-term memory activity called the *I*.

Though cognizer theory does not as yet provide a completely satisfactory account for the concept of mind, it does provide a common place for empirical information to amass. The mind goes though changes, but the ability to identify these changes with brain states does not, in and of itself, provide grounds for choosing between different philosophies of the mind. If people can precisely explain what ties together brain states and catalog extensively the psychological changes that go along with them, then there will still remain the question of whether the mind is simply a collection of those changes or whether it acts to produce them.

Cognizer theory does not side with any particular view about the metaphysical status of the *I*. Made immediately and without any sort of inference, mental statements are merely expressions of inner physical states. The mind is a private realm, to be sure, but so is the neural activity that stimulates it. The outside world impinges on the senses, evoking perceptions that are stored away as a unique internal representation associated with all the other experiences one has had. The neural mixing pot where activity evoked by current experience meets activity recalled from memory is called the *I*.

The *I* is that bundle of perceptions that were so clear and distinct to philosophers from Descartes on. As we have seen, its cause is a pattern of neural activity. The *I* is enduring, continuous through time, even during sleep, because its memories still endure. Without the memories, the *I* loses its individuality. Outside observers will still identify an *I* with a certain body, but to the individuals themselves, it is memory that determines who one is.

As Bishop Berkeley pointed out, all that people can know for sure is their perceptions. The fact that those perceptions can now be correlated with brain states does not affect one bit the problem of whether one's perceptions indicate a material world that defies religion, or at the other extreme, a realm of thought that exists only in the mind of God. Between these two extremes lies a whole universe of speculation that is consistent with cognizer theory.

9

Biotechnology Unleashed

Machines Modeled after Man

Since ancient times, physicians, biologists, psychologists, and a number of others have attempted to attain a detailed understanding of human intelligence. It took, however, a synthesis of biology and high technology to finally come up with blueprints for intelligent machines modeled on the brain. Cognizers — machines modeled on nature's own design for mankind — have unleashed the biotechnology theorists' wildest dreams.

■▄▄▄ Since the dawn of mankind, people have been inventors. The list of mankind's innovations that have fundamentally changed global society is continually growing. Mastery of fire, the wheel, the plow, gunpowder, the telephone, the automobile, the computer—all these and more have transformed the world in which we live for better or worse, and the pace of change is increasing rapidly.

Cognizers could become another world-changing technology—synthetic beings modeled on nature's own designs, automata that are not merely artificially intelligent but harbor the same kind of natural intelligence that we do, because they are designed on the same plan.

Before the computer was invented, *computer* was the title of a job that involved calculations. The word yielded its meaning to electronic computers only after the patterns of pencil-and-paper calculations had been automated by machinery. *Cognizer* was a word once used to pay a compliment to a particularly intelligent person, but now refers to machines that attempt to mimic thought.

Cognizers, whether flesh and blood or cast in metal and microchips, exhibit basic intelligence. The metallic ones may be synthetic, but their intelligence is genuine. And these new machines are intelligent for precisely the same reason that human cognizers are intelligent: because they are designed from the ground up to emulate the brain and nervous system.

An understanding of how cognizers work, invigorating in its own right, can lead to a deeper understanding of oneself. The builders of these machines are attempting to understand how mankind deals with everyday problems. Then, with microchip circuitry, they recast the intelligent operations employed in those solutions into machines that perform the same function.

This better understanding of the brain and nervous system is ringing in an astounding new age. Already cognizers are emerging from the research laboratories to tackle jobs that digital computers are ill-equipped to handle, such as learning a language just by listening to it, reading written text, or perceiving objects from a bundle of raw sensation.

Also, cognizers will be user friendly in a way that digital computers are not because they will learn human languages rather than imposing a foreign computer language on people. Anyone who has used a computer knows that half the job is telling the computer what to do in its own private language. When those instructions are the slightest bit off, the whole program can go haywire. Cognizers, on the other hand, can not have bugs in their software because they use no software. Cognizers eliminate the need for programming by learning just as people do. This ability also means that cognizers can adapt to novel situations, freeing their users from the burden of having to work out in advance solutions for every possible problem.

Cognizers, like human brains, are devoid of computer circuitry, making the word *biocomputing* a misnomer. The brain does not compute—does not deduce perfect conclusions from available evidence according to the rules of logic. Cognizers, like human brains, do not deduce conclusions, but jump to them. This characteristic leaves open the possibility that both cognizers and brains will make mistakes, but humanity has managed to thrive for millennia in spite of this possibility.

The distinction between what the mind does during cognition and what the computer does during calculation is striking on many counts. Computers separate the functions of remembering and computing, placing one in its semiconductor memories and the other in the central processing unit (CPU). Cognizers, on the other hand, combine the memory and processing through principles such as association, generalization, optimization, self-organization, and categorization. In this way, cognizers transcend the bottleneck between the memory and CPU that is choking traditional computers.

But blurring the distinction between memory and processing does not mean we should blur our *thinking* about that distinction. Although cognizers distribute a representation of individual objects throughout a network of analog-processing nodes that are highly interconnected, they are not distributing computation among those nodes. Rather, cognizers appear to be harnessing the forces of mathematical chaos to arrive at conclusions without computation. Since this difference means that a computer is still better at calculations and rote memory functions than a cognizer, the one may never replace the other, because they are based on different information-processing principles.

Another reason cognizers will not displace computers is that computers cannot make sloppy logical mistakes. A computer is explicitly programmed with the rules of logic and must follow those rules, right or wrong. Perhaps the best cognizer system will be a *neurocomputer,* a hybrid in which a computer checks a cognizer for logical mistakes, and a cognizer keeps the computer from irrelevant tangents.

Cognizer Applications Are Endless

The computer revolution is being literally vitalized—that is, made lifelike—by cognizers modeled after nature's own design for mankind. By mimicking the brain and nervous system, cognizers serve as the missing link that could actualize the dream of a genuine synthetic intelligence. This synthetic intelligence would be as different from today's artificial intelligence as a synthetic steak made from soybeans is different from an artificial steak made of wax.

> "Find me a novel depicting the typical emotional pact between loving partners in seventeenth-century France," a late-rising student on the way to the shower calls to his cognizer.

"Yes sir, I am confident I can have that for you in approximately 10 minutes and . . ."

"Cut the chatter and get to work," says the student, slamming the bathroom door.

Fifteen minutes later, he emerges. "Cognizer, what have you got?"

"I have located a delightful novel called—."

"Just give me a printout—a short passage of dialog between the two lovers that sums up their relationship."

"But sir, I took the trouble to polish my French accent while you shaved and am prepared to read to you the most beautiful passage—"

"Sorry, got no time this morn." The student rips off the printout and runs down the hall toward class. "And don't forget to make that plane reservation for spring break."

To get a computer to behave in such a manner would require a volume of software larger than any now amassed and a processor about the size of Venus. Yet, if cognizers develop as quickly as computers did before them, then such a scene may be possible in the near future.

Even with cognizers in their present, poorly developed state, they are being applied to everything from handwriting recognition to advising stockbrokers to choosing routing paths for cellular telephone systems. Cognizers could easily revolutionize society as did the wheel, the steam engine, and the computer before them.

Out from Academia

It was at the universities that theories on the nervous system were born, but such theories are now moving out into the marketplace. An early explorer from academia was Leon Cooper, who has expanded his responsibilities as professor at Brown University to found Nestor. Cooper, who received the Nobel prize for his work on superconductivity, has created what he calls a universal learning system. His technique has been painstakingly adapted to real-world problems and has proven itself in areas as diverse as handwriting recognition and financial analysis. In 1988, Nestor built more working systems for application areas than any other company. Its clients read like a Who's Who in industry, ranging from Chemical Bank to Ford Motor Company.

As a result of a raft of engineering development systems that became available in 1987, other cognizers are poised to enter the commercial marketplace. These machines are being used by manufacturing companies to craft quickly commercial products based on living nervous systems.

These first-generation engineering development systems were built quickly by simulating cognizers with digital computer circuitry to form neurocomputers. One startup company, the Hecht-Nielsen Neurocomputer, pioneered this approach and even supplies a month-long course with its neural network simulators. Hecht-Nielsen offers a software version of Stephen Grossberg's adaptive resonance theory, ART.

Other startup companies are following suit by wiring plug-in modules or specialized software for personal computers that add cognizing simulation abilities. Companies such as NeuralWare (Sewickley, PA), Neural Systems (Vancouver, B.C., Canada), Neuronics (Cambridge, MA), AI Ware (Cleveland, OH), Dair Computer Systems (Palo Alto, CA), and Excalibur Technologies (Albuquerque, NM) are having to fight over the limited number of experts available in the field. The field requires a special kind of researcher, an engineer who is also familiar with the neural networks of the brain. Since the principles on which the brain operates are fundamentally different from traditional human-engineered machines, few people are experts in both fields. Yet, as the field becomes established, the number of experts will increase to meet the growing demand.

Cognizer research is not confined to startups. Industrial giants like AT&T and TRW are also making big investments in large-scale systems that perform tasks for which conventional computers are proving inadequate. TRW has taken a straightforward approach in solving target-recognition problems for specific defense projects with large, expensive cognizers. AT&T

is taking the opposite tack by building small, inexpensive microchips that emulate the nervous system. Medium-sized companies are also getting into the act. For instance, Scientific Applications International, a defense contractor, has crafted an engineering development system that combines a desktop personal computer with simulation software and a plug-in accelerator. Japanese developers, such as NEC, Fujitsu, and NHK Laboratories, are also planning for hybrid cognizer/computers—neurocomputers. They feel that computers must be slowly augmented with cognizers over the next 20 years in order to transcend the limitations of computation.

But innovative entrepreneurs around the world are leaping ahead to build genuine cognizing microchips. Synaptics, for instance, has combined the talents of two microchip innovators who have already made their marks on the electronics industry—Carver Mead, who pioneered the methods behind today's superdense microchips, and Federico Faggin, who received the Marconi Award for his part in inventing the world's first microprocessor at Intel.

Synaptics' microchips attempt to mimic the human senses. By studying the biological sensory apparatus and mirroring it in microchips, Synaptics is building hardware that can act as the eyes and ears of advanced recognition systems. In Japan, Asahi Chemical Industry Company has taken the leading role by building a speech-recognition system based on Helsinki University of Technology professor Teuvo Kohonen's circuitry. Kohonen modeled his creations on the ear/brain system.

Professional Organization Support

Though AT&T has held private conferences on the subject since 1983, it was not until 1986 and 1987 that the study of electronic applications of neural networks was sanctioned by the National Science Foundation (NSF) and the Institute of Electrical and Electronic Engineers (IEEE). The NSF held its first conference, *Neural Networks and Neuromorphic Systems,* in Waltham, MA on

October 7–8, 1986, and the IEEE held two conferences in 1987. *The First Annual International Conference On Neural Networks* (June 21–24, 1987) was endorsed by the San Diego, CA, IEEE section, and an IEEE workshop on *Neural Information Processing Systems—Natural and Synthetic* was held in Denver, CO, on November 8–12, 1987. Other professional organizations, such as the American Association for Artificial Intelligence (AAAI), have held specific lectures on building machines like the brain, but the NSF and IEEE meetings were the first open meetings dedicated to the subject. In 1988 the annual IEEE meetings were joined by *nEuro '88—the First European Conference on Neural Networks,* June 6–8, 1988, in Paris, and the first annual meeting of the newly formed *International Neural Network Society,* on September 6–10, 1988, in Boston.

The amount of research still needed to understand the brain is large, and our areas of ignorance are vast. But, the questions are well understood, research is ongoing, and the field is growing. It is only a matter of time before cognizers move from being an academic curiosity to being a part of everyday life.

Epilogue

I intended this chapter to be the introduction,
but later decided that it gave away too much too early.
If you must rush to the conclusion,
this summary will do.

R. C. J.

An impending computer crisis has stimulated many researchers in government and industry to try to build machinery that emulates the human nervous system more closely. Early in this century, the computer revolution originated from an oversimplified model of a nerve cell. Because neurons generate pulses that are either *on* or *off*, early technologists believed that they emulated the 1s and 0s of digital computers. Armed with this misconception, computer researchers thought they were building electronic brains.

Though the digital computer has enjoyed immense success, computer scientists eventually ran up against their inherent limit. John von Neumann's most enduring contribution to computer design has turned out to be the design's limiting factor—a program stored in memory separate from a central processing unit. Because a central processing unit could be programmed with instructions stored in a separate memory unit, the same computer could handle completely different types of problems. This ability made the digital computer extremely adaptable, but has also bred the two major flaws of von Neumann's design: Someone has to explicitly adapt the computer—program it—for each new problem, and the path between memory and the processor was a bottleneck. The complexity of computer programs and the traffic between processor and memory have grown steadily worse as computers have become more powerful.

Today, computer scientists have pushed digital technology to its limit. The path between the processor and memory has been shortened to the point that it has reached the limits imposed by the fundamental laws of nature. Recent breakthroughs like superconductivity—the resistanceless conduction of electrical current—will help computers push even closer to these theoretical limits, but even these advances are not enough.

The other flaw, that somebody must figure out the right sequence of instructions to load into the memory unit, has also run up against the fundamental limits of human organization. The computer programs proposed to run Star Wars, for instance, involve millions of lines of code that no one person can ever wholly comprehend. The dependability of these programs can never be verified except by committee, a prospect that instills little confidence.

To cure this crisis, bold new computer designs are being proposed almost daily. The most ambitious of these undertakings, perhaps the Connection Machine from Thinking Machines, attempts to transcend the von Neumann bottleneck by harnessing 64,000 tiny but separate microprocessors simultaneously. Thus, rather than trying to build a faster and faster one-processor computer, massive numbers of slower microprocessors are interconnected to form a larger parallel processor.

When these designs were implemented, however, their creators soon discovered that the problem of interconnecting and programming such massive numbers of microcomputers is even harder than managing a single, very fast one. The prospect for building a machine as complex as the brain appeared to be impossible. The brain has approximately 100 billion neurons with 10,000 connections each, for a rough average of 1,000,000 billion units of information in less than a cubic foot. A digital memory of that capacity today would fill 1,000 washing machine-sized cabinets. Clearly, the brain is not built on the digital model.

Computers divide their efforts between calculating and remembering. Their program of instructions acts on stored memories of numbers and symbols. Parallel processors multiply this type of operation by the number of processing units they use. Cognizers, on the other hand, dispense with the distinction between calculating and remembering by using only a single type of unit. Because cognizers learn instead of following a program of instructions, they can be adapted for a given problem simply by adding units.

For example, instead of buying a computer with 1,000,000 units of memory and loading that memory with programs, you could use a cognizer with 1,000 units and 100,000 connections that can learn on its own. Even if you have a parallel processor with this number of units, each unit contains a single processor that acts on each element in a memory one step at a time. A cognizer uses all of its units and connections simultaneously, thereby gaining a speed advantage.

Cognizers also tolerate faults better than computers. When a memory element of a computer fails, it can often cause a major malfunction. But with cognizers, each piece of information is stored in the network as a whole, not in any individual memory location. This ability makes cognizers inherently fault tolerant since damage to a part of the synthetic neural network simply decreases its memory capacity slightly without interfering with its functioning. Like a holographic image, all the information is stored everywhere in the cognizer's circuitry.

Cognizers Need Their Sleep

Because their memory and communication methods are like the brain's, cognizers can almost be said to bridge the gap between man and machine. Some researchers have even suggested that cognizers, like men, have need for sleep and dreams. One such suggestion has come from pioneering researcher John Hopfield.

Hopfield's synthetic neural circuitry stores and recalls memories using a phenomenon that is common to many physical processes—energy minimization. All physical processes tend to wind down: Sand falls to the bottom of the hour glass, water runs downhill, and the jittering molecules of a liquid tend to settle down and cool over time. Hopfield's simplifying innovation was to build an electronic circuit that performs logical functions merely by energy relaxation. A circuit that can be taught a number of memories has been built on this principle, but Hopfield has found that to keep the memories straight, the circuit must be induced to sleep and dream.

Some psychologists believe that during sleep, an unlearning process takes place in which the experiences of the day are merged with existing memories via dreaming and then released from the forefront of consciousness. Hopfield, a physicist, was prompted to speculate on such a psychology of the mind because, in his experiments with cognizing circuitry, he found that a process similar to sleeping and dreaming was periodically required. Lack of sleep in humans will eventually overload the brain so that it is difficult to think clearly and remember events easily. In extreme cases of sleep deprivation, humans will even begin to hallucinate. Hopfield discovered that his circuits also began to behave sluggishly and elicit unintended responses, similar to hallucinations, when continuously exercised. When he induced a process that he likened to sleep, however, his circuits perked up and behaved normally again until they needed another sleep session. He induced this sleep state by purposefully causing his circuits to elicit spurious memories—a patchwork of memories combined from unrelated events to create absurd pseudoexperiences.

The result of Hopfield's work is a circuit-wiring theory developed by a physicist with some help from biology to solve electronic problems. The hope is that the gross similarity Hopfield's networks bear to nature's networks will cause these microchips to exhibit other emergent qualities, perhaps even self-awareness. Some have speculated that a critical number of brain cells may be needed to exhibit self-consciousness. It is hoped that as their raw mass increases, these chips will develop such emergent qualities.

Psychology's Failure

The explanation of concepts like self-consciousness by psychologists is sadly lacking in quantifiable theory. A remarkable amount of laboratory data has been amassed since the late 1800s, when Ivan Pavlov discovered how learning by association works, but no psychologist has yet come up with an analytic theory to explain it.

The stark picture drawn by some of Pavlov's descendants—the psychological behaviorists—was that people were mere automata, programmed by their genes and environment. In their frustration at not finding a strictly deterministic theory, behaviorists have turned to statistically based theories that concentrate on categorization. Many such ad hoc theories quantify observations by picking a predefined set of mental and physical characteristics and then measuring the statistical relations among them by experimentation.

Using conventional programming techniques, traditional artificial intelligence researchers have attempted to build machines that have the characteristics of deterministic, logical-deduction systems—the behaviorist's unattainable ideal. Such approaches methodically force software engineers to instill their machines—expert systems—with abilities that represent a human expert's own conception of what they do and how they do it. In theory, by encoding an expert's knowledge in facts and rules, these AI researchers can produce a machine that can do the same job in the same way.

The flaw in this approach is that it ignores the first lesson of modern psychology—that a person's "logical" explanations for his or her behavior are largely a rationalization. The real reasons for behavior lie deep down among a mass of accumulated experiences, inherited impulses, and learned emotional responses. The real causes of wise decisions are inaccessible to the conscious mind. Many psychologists forget this elementary principle when they start talking about AI and try to present the macroscopic phenomena studied by cognitive psychology as the true description of how humans make decisions.

Such artificial intelligence theorists have built a structure without a foundation, because any human expert worth his salt does not know how he does what he does. The more skilled the expert, the more mysterious the expertise. For that reason, traditional approaches to AI are floating untethered above the vast amount of available experimental data amassed by Pavlov and his successors. This stubborn adherence to viewing intelligent behavior in high-flying intellectual terms has doomed traditional AI systems to mere mimicry.

In limited domains, AI's expert systems have found considerable success. For instance, Digital Equipment uses an expert system to calculate what cables are needed when a customer orders specific computer configurations. But when AI systems are taken out of such limited domains and asked to confront situations that are not clearly specified, they inevitably fail. At first, it was thought that domains could be gradually expanded until they were so large that they would suitably simulate an unbounded system. But the size of the domain quickly grows larger than the complexity of the phenomena the system is intended to emulate. Whenever an explanation threatens to become more complex than the phenomena it explains, it is time to search for a new one.

Thought versus Computation

For the first time, there are quantifiable theories that explain the action of thought. These theories may also clarify some age-old questions about consciousness itself. For instance, if one's short-term memory is filled with a mixture of resonances from the outside world and from long-term memory, then the chaotic nature of how these resonances react with one another may explain the free will that one experiences in an apparently deterministic world. If neural theorists are correct, it may be possible for scientific explanations to coexist with true freedom of the will.

A popular concept is that through science we will be able to determine and control the future, a concept which causes some people to view scientific advances with mixed feelings. This concept began with the gravitational theories of Newton and Galileo who described the world in terms of underlying physical principles that were completely deterministic. According to these principles, any given instant in the history of the world was precisely determined by the past and precisely determines the future.

At a deeply intuitive level, this airtight conception of reality is repulsive because people can directly experience freedom of choice, and scientific theories are now producing explanations that are consonant with this experience. For example, Heisenberg's uncertainty theory teaches that on the microscopic level, the exact location and velocity of objects cannot both be simultaneously determined. Taken together with the mathematics of chaos theory, these small discrepancies in initial conditions could naturally feed upon others, magnifying uncertainty to the macroscopic level.

These new theories, though, have not permeated the social sciences. Psychology has therefore become divided into movements that refuse even to read each other's results. Some psychologists attempt to deal with the full complexity of the mind, but then have to depart from accepted, scientific methods and theories. Others, like the behaviorists, attempt to reduce the human experience to a set of clearly defined operations that can be deterministically linked. Some psychologists and AI theorists claim that the rules and facts programmed into an organism— by genetics from inheritance and conditioning from the environment—fully describe and dictate behavior.

Still, the increasingly popular AI symbolic processors create only an artificial intelligence because they merely manipulate symbols according to rules. The problem of how those symbols can contain meaning is a serious barrier to further development of traditional AI techniques. Cognizers, though, have the same notion of meaning that humans do because they model the same processes of acquiring information from the world and recalling it from memory. Memories "mean" their proper objects precisely because the neural activity in short-term memory is similar to that caused by the object itself. Both are the same in kind—one from the object itself and the other from the memory of the object—and thus they can be directly compared.

Even an accurate model of perception and memory, however, is not enough to explain behavior. Emotion is the third ingredient necessary to distinguish living organisms from mere automata. Machines will follow the same course of action endlessly, or at least until they break down. Living organisms become bored with any repetitive behavior and do something else just for variety. Because emotions stimulate living beings to pursue unpredictable actions, they are vital to intellectual achievements. Without emotions to stimulate from the inside, men would learn the minimum necessary to survive and be satisfied. While the first wave of cognizers concentrates on emulating the thoughts of humans, more advanced work is turning to emotion.

Era of Sixth Generation

Cognizers are capitalizing on the way nature organizes its own systems. This approach is one step beyond the fifth generation of artificial intelligence and could herald a new era—a sixth generation that realizes the unfolding potential of electronic circuitry. Living organisms have evolved remarkably sensible measures for dealing with the world that high-technology systems are only now beginning to emulate. Living organisms can sense their environment and develop a unique, internal representation of it. That personal information base then helps them to learn, recognize, remember, think about, and create new strategies for coping with the world. A detailed understanding of these processes could result in technologies that achieve true machine intelligence.

Current technologies are attempting to mimic intelligence by using high-level structures derived from cognitive psychologists, but this endeavor is quickly running up against a brick wall. Because every possible circumstance must be programmed into such artificially-intelligent systems, they require not only enormous computing power, but a near-omniscient programming staff.

Truly intelligent, living organisms obviously do not suffer the same fate. Living things, by virtue of their private, internal representations of the world, can solve increasingly complex problems with virtually no additional programming because living organisms can learn. They exhibit what sixth generation scientists call *self-organization*. To be sure, genetics makes a paramount contribution to overall behavior, but learning is more important to the high-level decisions by which a conscious being judges its environment. Rather than conceive of every possible circumstance ahead of time, a self-organizing system learns to cope with novelty by changing its internal representation to match changing circumstances. By learning to mimic this technique, we will gain not only a fundamentally useful technology, but an understanding of ourselves as well.

Select Bibliography

Books

Arbib, Michael. *The Metaphorical Brain*. New York: Wiley-Interscience, 1972.

Feigenbaum, E.A., and J. Feldman. *Computers and Thought*. New York: McGraw-Hill, 1963.

Freeman, W.J. *Mass Action in the Nervous System*. New York: Academic Press, 1975.

Grossberg, S. ed. *The Adaptive Brain, I: Cognition, Learning, Reinforcement, and Rhythm*. Amsterdam: Elsevier, 1987.

Grossberg, S. *Studies of Mind and Brain*. Boston: Reidel Press, 1982.

Grossinger, Richard. *Embryogenesis: From Cosmos to Creature, the Origins of Human Biology*. Berkeley: North Atlantic Books, 1986.

Hebb, D.O. *The Organization of Behavior*. New York: Wiley, 1949.

Kant, Immanuel. *Critique of Pure Reason*. (Norman Kemp Smith, trans.) New York: St. Martins Press, 1965. (For easier reading see Kant entry in "Encyclopedia of Philosophy".)

Katz, Bernard. *Nerve, Muscle and Synapse*. New York: McGraw-Hill, 1966.

Kohonen, T. *Content Addressable Memories*. New York: Springer, 1980.

Minsky, M., and S. Papert. *Perceptrons: An Introduction to Computational Geometry*. Cambridge: MIT Press, 1969 (revised 1988).

Pregogine, Illya, and Isabelle Stengers. *Order out of Chaos*. New York: Bantam, 1986.

Rosenblatt, F. *Principles of Neurodynamics.* New York: Spartan Books, 1962.

Rumelhart, D.E., and J.L. McClelland. *Parallel Distributed Processing: Explorations in the Microstructure of Cognition.* Cambridge: MIT Press, 1985.

Shannon, C.E., and W. Weaver. *The Mathematical Theory of Communication.* Champaign, IL: University of Illinois Press, 1959.

Shepard, G. *The Synaptic Organization of the Brain.* New York: Oxford University Press, 1974.

Stevens, Leonard A., *Neurons—The Building Blocks of the Brain.* New York: Crowell, 1974.

Papers and Articles

Amari, Shun-ichi. "Neural Theory of Association and Concept Formation." *Biological Cybernetics* 26 (3) (1977): 175–85.

Anderson, James. "Memory Storage Model Utilizing Spatial Correlation Functions." *Kybernetik* 5 (1968): 113–19.

_____. "Cognitive and Psychological Computation with Neural Models." IEEE Trans. on Systems, Man and Cybernetics, Vol. SMC-135, (September/October 1983): 799–815.

_____. "Neural Models: Networks For Fun And Profit." *Nature,* 322, no. 6078 (July 31, 1986): 406–407.

_____. "Cognitive Capabilities of a Parallel System." In *Disordered Systems and Biological Organization,* edited by E. Bienenstock, 209–226. New York: Springer-Verlag, 1986.

Arbib, Michael. "Brain Theory and Cooperative Computation." *Human Neurobiology* 4 (1985): 201–18.

Athale, Ravi, Harold Szu, and Charles Friedlander. "Attentive Associative Memory and Its Optical Implementation." *Optics Letters* (July 1986).

Ballard, Dana. "Cortical Connections and Parallel Processing: Structure and Function." *Behavioral And Brain Sciences* 9 (1986): 67–102.

Brown, Chappell. "Chips Designed to Mimic Nervous System." *Electronic Engineering Times* (March 24, 1986): 61.

_____. "First Commercial Nerve Nets Challenge Traditional AI." *EE Times* (March 31, 1986): 1.

_____. "Hopfield's Nerve Nets Realize Biocomputing." *EE Times* (April 7, 1986): 59.

_____. "Neural Network Startups Backed by Venture Capital." *EE Times* (January 5, 1987): 23.

_____. "Learning to Replace Programming?" *EE Times* (March 31, 1987): 53.

Brown, Chappell, and R. Colin Johnson. "AT&T Seeks a Universal Parallel Processor Architecture." *EE Times* (March 17, 1987): 55.

_____. "Theories of Neural Nets Expose the Limits of AI." *EE Times* (June 22, 1987): 41.

Carpenter, G.A., and S. Grossberg. "A Massively Parallel Architecture for a Self-Organizing Neural Pattern Recognition Machine." *Computer Vision, Graphics and Image Processing* 37 (1987): 54–115.

El-Leithy, N., R.W. Newcomb, and M. Zaghloul. "A Basic MOS Neural-Type Junction and a Perspective on Neural-Type Microsystems." Proceedings of the First International Conference on Neural Networks (IEEE), San Diego, June 1987.

Freeman, Walter and Christine Skarda. "How Brains Make Chaos in Order to Make Sense of the World." *Behavioral and Brain Sciences* 10:2 (1987): 161–95.

Fukushima, K., and S. Miyake. "Neocognitron: A New Algorithm for Pattern Recognition Tolerant of Deformations and Shifts in Position." *Pattern Recognition* SMC-13, No. 5 (1984): 455–69.

Fukushima, K., S. Miyake, and T. Ito. "Neocognitron: A Neural Network Model for a Mechanism of Visual Pattern Recognition." *IEEE Trans. on Systems Man and Cybernetics* SMC–13 (September/October 1983): 826–34.

Gelperin, Alan, J. Hopfield, and D. Tank. "The Logic of LIMAX Learning." In *Model Neural Networks and Behavior*, New York: Plenum, 1985.

Grossberg, S. "Cortical Dynamics of Three-Dimensional Form, Color, and Brightness Perception, I: Monocular Theory," and "II: Binocular Theory." *Perception and Psychophysics* 41 (1987): 87–116; 117–58.

Hammerstrom, Dan, David Maier, and Shreekant Thakkar. "The Cognitive Architecture Project." *IEEE SigArch*, 14, no. (1) (January 1986): 9–21.

Hecht-Nielsen, Robert. "Performance Limits of Optical, Electro-Optical, and Electronic Neurocomputers." Internal paper at Hecht-Nielsen Neurocomputer Corporation, San Diego, CA.

Hinton, Geoffrey E. "Learning in Parallel Networks." *BYTE* (April 1985): 265–73.

Hopfield, John J. "Neural Networks and Physical Systems with Emergent Collective Computational Abilities." *Proceedings of the National Academy of Sciences* 79 (1982): 2554–58.

Hopfield, John, and David Tank. "Collective Computation in Neuronlike Circuits." *Scientific American* (December 1987): 104–14.

Johnson, R. Colin. *EE Times*,

"Neurons in Silicon." (April 18, 1988): 85.

"Thinking Big, Building Small." (April 11, 1988): 45.

"Neural Model: One Equation Does It All." (March 28, 1988): 53.

"Kohonen Consolidates Neural Net R&D." (March 21, 1988): 50.

"Beyond Detailed Modeling." (March 7, 1988): 43.

"Pondering the Perceptron." (February 22, 1988): 33.

"Nestor Frees Neural Nets from Hardware Chains." (February 1, 1988): 33.

"Optics and Neural Networks: Marriage of Convenience." (January 18, 1988): 41.

"Avoiding the AI Trap: Synthetic Intelligence." (January 4, 1988): 33.

"Lockheed Targets Neural Nets." (December 14, 1987): 51.

"Progress Report: Carver Mead and Silicon Ears." (December 7, 1987): 45.

"IEEE Puts Neural Nets into Focus." (November 30, 1987): 45.

"DARPA Orders Full Review of Neural Networks." (November 30, 1987): 46.

"Neural Nets to Arm NASA Space Robots?" (October 26, 1987): 49.

"Artificial Life: Electronic Frontier." (October 12, 1987): 41.

"Learning Modules Permit Scalable Neural Systems." (August 10, 1987): 53.

"Neural Networks Naive, Says Minsky." (August 3, 1987): 41.

"Learning: The Final Frontier for Automata." (April 29, 1987): 42.

"Code Words—The Problem with Artificial Intelligence." (April 13, 1987): 43.

"Neural Networks in Japan: Part 2." (April 6, 1987): 49.

"Japan Develops Neural Networks: Part I, Academia." (March 30, 1987): 35.

"Neural Net Speech Systems in Works." (March 23, 1987): 10.

"Japan's Sixth Generation Project: Striking a Fine Balance." (March 23, 1987): 33.

"Japan Opens Sixth Generation to All." (March 16, 1987): 1.

"Code Words—New Frontiers: When Is Chaos Not Random?" (February 2, 1987): 43.

"Neural Systems Make Comeback after Nearly 50-Year Gestation." (January 5, 1987): 22.

"Neural Network Chips Are Proving to Be Viable Challengers to AI Systems." (December 8, 1986): 58.

"Connectionist Researching Neural Nets." (September 8, 1986): 65.

"Brain-Emulating Circuits Need 'Sleep' and 'Dreams'." (April 7, 1986): 59.

"Nature Provides Architecture for Parallel Processing." (March 31, 1986): 53.

"Frankenstein Fable Becoming Fact." (March 24, 1986): 61.

"Nerve Nets Built on Chip." (March 24, 1986): 1.

Johnson, R. Colin. *Electronics,*

"Programs That Write Programs." (June 2, 1982): 129,

"Ada, The Ultimate Language?" (February 10, 1981): 127,

"Special Report: Microsystems and Software." (October 23, 1980): 150.

Johnson, R. Colin, and Chappell Brown. *EE Times,*

"Once Again, Designers' Thoughts Turn To Analog." (July 13, 1987): 41.

"Neural Networks Get A Conference To Call Their Own." (June 29, 1987): 39.

"Processor Mimics Memory." (May 25, 1987): 37.

"Engineer A Black-Box Solution In The First Real 'Cognizer' Contest." (May 4, 1987): 51.

Johnson, R. Colin, and E. Rosenfeld. "A Boost for Neural Pioneers." *EE Times.* (August 17, 1987): 47.

Johnson, R. Colin, and T. Schwartz. "BAM! A World's First in ElectroOptics Arrives." *EE Times* (October 5, 1987): 47.

Kirkpatrick, S., C.D. Gellat, and M.D. Vecchi. "Optimization by Simulated Annealing." *Science* 220 (1983): 671–80.

Lambe, John, A.P. Thakoor, Alex Moopen, and J.L. Lamb. "Binary Synaptic Memory Connections Based on a Si:H and SnOx:Sb." Proceedings of the Second Annual Conference on Neural Networks for Computing, American Institute of Physics, 1986.

Mead, Carver, M. Sivilotti, and M. Emerling. "A Novel Associative Memory Implemented Using Collective Computation." Chapel Hill Conference on VLSI, 1985.

Mead, Carver. "Silicon Models of Neural Computation." Proceedings of the IEEE First Annual International Conference on Neural Networks, San Diego, California, June 21–24, 1987.

Mead, Carver. "Plenary Remarks on the Function of the Ear." Proceedings of the IEEE Conference on Neural Information Processing Systems—Natural and Synthetic, Denver, CO November 8–12, 1987.

Psaltis, D., and N. Farhat. "Optical Information Processing Based on an Associative Memory Model of Neural Nets with Thresholding and Feedback." *Optics Letter* 10 (1985): 98–100.

Rhumelhart, D.E. and D. Zipser. "Feature Discovery by Competitive Learning." *Cognitive Science* 9 (1985): 75–112.

Rumelhart, David E., Geoffrey E. Hinton, and R.J. Williams. "Learning Internal Representations by Error Propagation." Institute for Cognitive Science Report 8506, UCSD, September 1985.

Von Neumann, John. "The General and Logical Theory of Automata." Hixon Symposium, Pasadena, CA, September 20, 1948.

Where to Write

Amari, Shun-ichi
University of Tokyo, Bunkyo-ku, Tokyo 113, Japan

Anderson, Dana
University of Colorado, Institute for Laboratory Astrophysics, Boulder, CO 80309

Anderson, James,
Brown University, Providence, RI 02192

Carpenter, Gail
Boston University, 11 Cummington St., Room 244, Boston, MA 02215

Cooper, Leon
Brown University, Physics Department, Providence, RI 02912

Dress, William
Oak Ridge National Laboratory, Instrumentation and Controls Division, Oak Ridge, TN 37831-6007

Freeman, Walter
University of California Berkeley, Department of Physiology-Anatomy, Berkeley, CA 94720

Fukushima, Kunihiko
NHK Laboratories, 1-10-11 Kinua, Setagaya-ku, Tokyo, 157, Japan

Grossberg, Stephen
Boston University, 111 Cummington, St., Room 244, Boston, MA 02215

Hecht-Nielsen, Robert
Hecht-Nielsen Neurocomputer Inc., 5893 Oberlin Dr., Suite 105, San Diego, CA 92121

Hirai, Yuzo
University of Tsukuba, Institute of Informaction Sciences and Electronics, Sakura, Niihari, Ibaraki 305, Japan

Cognizers

Hopfield, John
California Institute of Technology, Division of Chemistry, MS-164-30, Pasadena, CA 91125

Kohonen, Teuvo
Helsinki University of Technology, Rakentajanaukio 2C, Espoo, SF-02150, Finland

Kosko, Bart
Verac Inc., 9605 Scranton Rd., San Diego, CA 92121

Malsburg, Christoph von der
Max Planck Institute of Biophysics and Chemistry, P.O. Box 2841, Goettingen D-3400, W. Germany

Matsuo, Kazuhiro
Fujitsu Lt., IIAS-SIS, 17-25 Shinkamata 1-Chome, Tokyo, Ohta-ku, 144, Japan

Okajima, Kenji
NEC Corp., Fundamental Research Labs, 4-1-4 Miyazaki 4-Chome, Miyamae-ku, Kanagawa 213, Japan

Psaltis, Demetri
California Institute of Technology, Department of Electrical Engineering, Pasadena, CA 91125

Szu, Harold
Naval Research Laboratory, MS-5750, Washington, DC 20375

Tank, David
AT&T Bell Labs, 600 Mountain Ave., Room 1C456, Murray Hill, NJ 07974

Touretzky, David
Carnegie-Mellon University, Computer Science Department, Pittsburgh, PA 15213

Widrow, Bernard
Stanford University, Durand Building, Room 139, Stanford, CA 94305

For information about cognizers write:
the Cognizer Connection
333 South State St.
Suite V-141
Lake Oswego, OR 97034

Index

Cognizers